LIVING
COURAGEOUSLY

LIVING
COURAGEOUSLY

You Can Face Anything, Just Do It Afraid

JOYCE MEYER

FaithWords

NEW YORK · BOSTON · NASHVILLE

Unless otherwise noted Scriptures are taken from *The Amplified Bible* (AMP). *The Amplified Bible, Old Testament,* copyright © 1965, 1987 by The Zondervan Corporation. *The Amplified New Testament,* copyright © 1954, 1958, 1987 by The Lockman Foundation. Used by permission.

Scripture quotations noted ASV are taken from the *American Standard Version.*

Scripture quotations noted NIV are taken from the *New International Version.* Copyright © 1973, 1978, 1984, by International Bible Society. Used by permission of Zondervan Publishing House. All rights reserved.

Scripture quotations noted NLT are taken from the *Holy Bible,* New Living Translation, Copyright © 1996. Used by permission of Tyndale House Publishers, Inc., Wheaton, Illinois 60189. All rights reserved.

Scripture quotations noted KJV are taken from the *King James Version* of the Bible.

Scripture quotations noted NKJV are taken from the *New King James Version.* Copyright © 1979, 1980, 1982 by Thomas Nelson, Inc. Publishers.

FaithWords
Hachette Book Group
1290 Avenue of the Americas
New York, NY 10104

www.faithwords.com

Printed in the United States of America

RRD-C

Originally published in hardcover by Hachette Book Group
First trade paperback edition: November 2015

10 9 8 7 6 5 4 3 2 1

FaithWords is a division of Hachette Book Group, Inc.
The FaithWords name and logo is a trademark of Hachette Book Group, Inc.

The Hachette Speakers Bureau provides a wide range of authors for speaking events. To find out more, go to www.hachettespeakersbureau.com or call (866) 376-6591.

The publisher is not responsible for websites (or their content) that are not owned by the publisher.

LCCN: 2014007464

ISBN 978-1-4555-1749-7 (pbk.)

CONTENTS

Fear! Has it ever been a problem for you? Has it ever held you back from moving into areas that could enrich your own life and the lives of others? I am sure your honest answer is yes because everyone is visited by fear at some time or another. Keep this in mind: If you have ever dealt with fear, or if you are dealing with fear now, you are not alone. Fear is one of the biggest problems that we all must face if we truly want to live life to its fullest.

But I have good news for you—there is a solution to fear!

One of the many benefits available to Christians is freedom from fear. But in order to receive that freedom, we have to be prepared to face fear head-on. When we avoid making changes or confronting issues in our lives because of fear or dread, we need to remember that God has promised to go before us and bring us through victoriously as we obey Him. I believe a close relationship with God is the solution to living boldly instead of fearfully.

> *I sought (inquired of) the Lord and required Him [of neces-sity and on the authority of His Word], and He heard me, and delivered me from all my fears.*
>
> Psalm 34:4

Throughout God's Word we are instructed not to fear. The statement "fear not" is found continuously throughout the Bible. God did not expect His children not to feel fear, nor to never be confronted by fear, but He does expect us not to submit to fear. We can and should resist it in the power of God. We are called by God to live courageously, boldly, and obediently—none of which is possible unless we are willing to recognize and deal with our fears.

Courage is not the absence of fear; it is fear that has said its prayers and decided to go forward anyway. I was tormented emotionally and prevented from doing many of the things that I wanted to do for many years simply because I was waiting to not feel afraid, but then I discovered that I could "do it afraid." You see, the freedom we have in Christ is that we can do anything we need to do because He is with us. He has gone before us and paved the way, and He promises to never leave us nor forsake us. It doesn't matter how we feel; we can boldly go forward in faith, trusting God. When we confront our fears with faith in God, we might still feel the effects of those fears, but they cannot stop us. Fear must eventually bow its knee to courage—it has no other choice.

The different types of fear are so numerous that I doubt they could even be counted, but they all have the same solution: Put your faith in God and go forward doing what He instructs you to do. God's power is available to us and is received through faith. Faith takes a step and believes that God will meet it with the power to follow through. As the Israelites traveled toward the Promised Land, they found themselves with the Red Sea blocking their way and the fierce Egyptian army rapidly coming up behind them. They felt afraid and began to complain, wishing they had never left Egypt at all. *Moses told the people, Fear not; stand still (firm, confident, undismayed) and see the salvation of the Lord which He will work for you today* (Exodus 14:13). In the midst of what seemed to be an impossible situation, God told Moses to go forward, lift up his rod, and stretch it out over the Red Sea and part it.

Moses had to take a step of obedience while still feeling afraid before he witnessed the miracle-working power of God doing the impossible. I wonder how foolish and afraid Moses felt when he stood with a rod in his hand holding it out over the water. What a foolish action it must have seemed to be in the face of such a huge dilemma, and yet the Red Sea did part and the Israelites crossed over safely, while God simultaneously destroyed the enemy that had caused them to feel fear in the first place. This was indeed a true miracle but one that would not have occurred unless Moses and the Israelites had been willing to "do it afraid."

Please don't miss this very important point: We take a step to be obedient to God while we feel afraid, and then that releases the grace (power) of God to do what needs to be done.

If you are looking for a way to never *feel* afraid again, then this book won't help you. But if you are ready to say good-bye to fear and learn to live courageously, I believe you will receive the spiritual tools you need to do so. It is your inherited right as a child of God to live life to the fullest and to enjoy it. Be expectant as you begin your journey to learn to conquer fear and be all God wants you to be, so you can do all that He wants you to do.

LIVING
COURAGEOUSLY

PART 1

I have divided the teaching in this book into two parts. In Part 1, I want to give you an understanding of what fear is, where it comes from, what your attitude toward it should be, and how you can overcome it.

CHAPTER 1

Say Good-Bye to Fear

The Lord is on my side; I will not fear. What can man do to me?

Psalm 118:6

Dear Fear,

I only refer to you as "dear" because of our long-term, intimate relationship, and certainly not because you are dear to me in any way. In fact, you have been a tormenting influence from start to finish. You have told me lies and prevented me from doing the things I wanted to do and should have done. You are indeed a miserable, wretched companion and one that I no longer am willing to be involved with.

I am writing you this letter to let you know that from this point forward, I will not fear! Although I may feel your presence, I will not bow down to your demands. I have a friend whose name is Jesus, and He has promised to never leave me nor forsake me, but to be with me always. He is indeed a powerful friend, and although you do have some power, His is by far much greater than yours. You can come against me, but Jesus lives in me, and the power of the one who is in me is greater than you are (see 1 John 4:4).

Although I cannot prevent you from coming to visit, I do want to give you notice that you will be ignored. I am far too busy now fellowshipping with my friend Jesus and developing an intimate relationship with Him to give you any of my time. The more time I spend with Jesus the more courageous I become. He is teaching me a new way to live, one that is exciting and adventurous—one that is fearless.

I also want to inform you that since I have so much experience with you and know how self-defeating it is to listen to you, I now intend to tell as many people as I can what a thief and a liar you are. The years I have wasted with you will be redeemed and I will bear much good fruit. Thank you for driving me to Jesus. You see, you made me so miserable that I sought a way to be free from you, and Jesus met me where I was and set me free.

Should you decide to waste your time and try to visit me even after my letter, I am letting you know ahead of time that you will be met by faith in God and a determination that I *will not fear!!*

Sincerely and determined,

_____

(place your name here)

I Will Not Fear

Before we can really begin dealing with specific types of fear and how to overcome them, I believe each reader needs to make a decision, and that decision is "I will not fear." It is necessary to have your mind set that you are done with fear. If you have been married to fear, it is time for a divorce! Time to cut off all ties and put yourself in a position where you are free to live the life you truly desire. One of obedience to God that will produce joy and promote growth and progress.

As you go through this book, you will learn about the nature and source of fear, the types of fear that people deal with, and how to resist it in the power of God, but first you need to make a firm decision that you are done with it. Your decision won't prevent fear from visiting you, but you are determining ahead of time that when it does, you will not give in to it. You only have one gear now, and that is forward! Fear holds us back, reversing us, but that gear is being stripped from our lives and all systems are now go!

The Word of God teaches us that we are to set our minds and keep them set on things above, not on things of the earth (see Colossians 3:2). When applying this verse to the subject of fear, we might say to set your mind and keep it set on faith in God's direction for your life, and not on fear that drives you backward or keeps you frozen in place, unable to make progress of any kind.

What I call "holy determination" is a good thing. It is not a determination of man's will only—which is not strong enough to finish the task—but a determination in and with God that you will not give up until you experience victory. Apart from Jesus, we can do nothing. Not even the strongest willpower will bring lasting success without Him. But with, in, and through Him, we can face anything and do anything that is His will for us.

The psalmist David often said, "I will not fear." I believe he said that as an answer to fear when it came knocking on the door of his mind and emotions. He was declaring his position in God and letting it be known that he intended to stand firm and not give in to the torment, lies, and threats of fear. He even went so far as to say that even if he walked through the valley of death, that he would fear no evil, for God was with him (see Psalm 23:4). David was setting his mind and keeping it set.

It would have been nice if fear did not exist, but God arranges things in such a way that we must always make a choice. He doesn't want robots that serve Him because they have no other choice; He desires that we freely choose Him and His ways. God has given us free will. That is a privilege and a responsibility. Every day we make lots of choices, and those choices determine the quality of life we will have. God shows us the best way to choose, but He will never coerce us to make the ones He desires us to make. Satan uses tactics of force and manipulation, but God gives us wisdom and the opportunity to choose right or wrong. In a way, we might say that God has made us the master of our own destiny. He wants us to use our will to choose His will, and when we do, the destiny He has in mind for us will come to pass.

However, should a person choose to use his own will to not follow God's will, God won't force him to do right. It is the person's choice.

> I call heaven and earth to witness this day against you that I have set before you life and death, the blessings and the curses; therefore choose life, that you and your descendants may live...
>
> Deuteronomy 30:19

It is easy to see from this Scripture that although we are confronted with good and evil (faith and fear), God wants us to choose faith in Him. Fear always brings death and curses, while faith brings life and blessings. I would venture to say that every decision we face in life fits into this Scripture in some way or another. Every decision we make provides life or death, blessings or curses. Even if a person decides to not get enough sleep and to have a diet of junk food, they are choosing death and curses instead of life and blessings. Ultimately a person is the culmination of the choices he has made in life.

Some decisions have more serious consequences than others do, but they all produce some level of consequence. God puts it very simply when He says that "we reap what we sow" (see Galatians 6:7). The result of bad choices can be overturned by making good choices, and so we see that man is never in a position where he cannot see positive change if he truly wants it. If you are tired of fear and its consequences, you can turn your life around by listening to what God is trying to say to you right now.

The decision is yours to make. Will you say good-bye to fear and not look back? Will you face life boldly knowing that God is always with you? Will you stop living by feelings and start living by the truth of God's Word? I believe that you will!

Deciding in advance that you will not live in fear helps you be prepared to meet it head-on when it comes.

Don't Run

When God told any of His servants to "fear not," He was in essence telling them that fear was going to attack them, and when it did, they were to remain steadfast and not run. Fear pressures us to run, hide, and watch life pass us by. Even in the Garden of Eden, as soon as Adam and Eve knew they had disobeyed God, their first instinct was to run away and hide from Him. God had intended them to live boldly, to rule and reign, but they were hiding.

After God created Adam and Eve, He blessed them and told them to be fruitful and multiply and fill the earth. He said they were to subdue it and have dominion over it and everything else He had created (see Genesis 1:28). That certainly doesn't sound like cowardice and timidity was His will for the man and woman He created. However, when they disobeyed God's command not to eat of the tree of the knowledge of good and evil, bringing sin into Earth's atmosphere, fear came with it. They could no longer stand boldly and comfortably in God's presence because they knew their actions were wrong, so they hid in fear. Sadly, mankind has been hiding in fear ever since.

Eventually, God sent His Son Jesus to set us free from sin and the fear it brings with it, but multitudes still reject God's beautiful answer found in Christ and continue to live defeated lives, hiding and running and being tormented by fears of all kinds. Make a decision that you will face issues squarely with God by your side. I have been saying for a long time that "the only way out is through." We cannot conquer anything by running away from it or trying to avoid it—we must go through it, and once we are safely on the other side, we have a victory that cannot be taken from us.

I tried for years to avoid my problems and the things from my past that were haunting me, but I finally decided to face them. It wasn't easy, but now that I am on the other side of them, I can certainly say that it was worth it.

I had to face the truth that my parents did not—and never could—truly love me because they didn't know what real love was. I had to squarely face that my father sexually, mentally, and verbally abused me, and my mother abandoned me in the situation by living in fear and refusing to confront my father. My childhood had been stolen and I could never get it back, but I could trust God to redeem it.

My mother's fear opened a door for many years of misery for

me, and it eventually destroyed her mental health and left her with only regrets for memories. Fear is NEVER a good choice. It has negative consequences that are life altering. I had to face these sad facts and trust God to work good out of them rather than allowing them to destroy me. But the first step toward victory was setting aside the fear of them and facing my life as it was, not as I wished it had been. I confronted it! I embraced it and went through to victory, and you can do the same thing no matter what your circumstances have been so far in life. Don't run from the truth and live in pretense, but instead choose to be honest, open, and not afraid of your past or your current reality.

There are several good examples in the Bible of men and women of God who ran from their circumstances or the will of God, and without fail, they all ended up back at the place they had run from. It is evidence that we never really get away from things by running from them. The truth is that they continue chasing us, and the only way to be free is to stop running, turn and face them boldly, and go all the way through to victory with God's help.

Jonah, a mighty prophet of God, did not want to do what God was asking him to do, so he ran and went the exact opposite direction from the one that God had instructed him to go in. He ended up in very bad circumstances and eventually prayed to God for help. As a result, God sent Jonah back to the place he ran from with the same instruction God gave him before he disobeyed and invited bad circumstances and misery into his life. The simple truth is that God is wiser than we are, and doing things His way is always the best policy. We can ignore that truth and go our own way, but we all eventually must come face-to-face with the result of our choices. Thank God that it is never too late to begin again! Jonah did repent and was able to begin again, and so can we.

Giving in to fear alters God's best plan for your life. Instead of being fearful, be obedient and do what He wants you to do, even if you have to *do it afraid!* The rewards are great.

Elisabeth Elliot, whose husband was killed along with four other missionaries in Ecuador, says that her life was completely controlled by fear. Every time she started to step out to minister, fear stopped her. Then a friend told her something that set her free. Her friend said, "Why don't you do it afraid?"

Do you see the power in that sentence? Her friend didn't say, "Maybe you should give up because you feel afraid" or "You're a weak Christian because you're dealing with fear." Her friend suggested that she trust God and press through the fear that she was feeling.

Elisabeth listened and took that advice, and alongside Rachel Saint, the sister of one of the murdered missionaries, they went on to evangelize the Indian tribes of Ecuador, including the very people who had killed their loved ones.

What an amazing story. I can only imagine the fear that Elisabeth felt each time she tried to go back to the place where her husband had been murdered. I am sure the images that Satan presented to her imagination were frightening, and the thoughts that he presented to her mind could have been disabling had she not decided that she was going to do the will of God even if she had to do it while she felt afraid.

She could have easily run, but she would have missed the amazing opportunity that God gave her to turn her husband's sacrifice into something good and beautiful. Courage will always defeat fear if we will let it guide us.

If you want to run, don't run away from things, run toward them. That is exactly what David did when he faced the giant, Goliath. God's Word states that David ran quickly toward the battle line. He did run, but he ran in the right direction. As we know from Scripture, David, against all sane and reasonable odds, did defeat Goliath and go on to become the king, champion, and hero of Israel. David was the least likely of all in the land at that time to be chosen for this task, but God doesn't see as man sees. God looks on the heart, and He saw that the little shepherd boy, David, had courage in his heart. David was untrained and uneducated in the ways of war, but an uneducated, untrained man with courage and faith in God is more valuable to Him than a highly educated, well-trained coward.

> *If you want to run, don't run away from things, run toward them.*

I have been privileged by God to lead a ministry that reaches a majority of the world with the Gospel of Jesus Christ. I would have been the least likely candidate. I did not have the right education, experience, or personality for the job, but I was willing to step out and try as long as God stayed with me. I know there were many others more naturally qualified than I was, and perhaps God gave them the opportunity even before He gave it to me, but they were afraid to believe or too afraid of failure to even try. I don't know why God chose me, but I do know that it certainly wasn't because I was qualified by natural standards.

God Is with You

Many of the men and women recorded in the Bible said the same thing as they faced challenges in their lives: "I will not fear because God is with me." How beautifully simple! They didn't require any advance proof of success or victory; they simply believed they could not fail because God was with them. It isn't hard to believe—even a child can do it.

A mother and her little four-year-old daughter were preparing to retire for the night. The child was afraid of the dark, and the mother, alone with the child, felt fearful also. When the light was out, the child caught a glimpse of the moon outside the window. "Mother," she asked, "is the moon God's light?" "Yes," said the mother. "God's light is always shining." The next question was, "Will God blow out His light and go to sleep?" And the mother replied, "No, my child. God never goes to sleep." Then out of the simplicity of a child's faith, the little girl said that which gave reassurance to the fearful mother: "Well, so long as God is awake, I am not afraid."[1]

No wonder Jesus said that we must believe as a little child.

God is surely with you and me, and because He is, we can do whatever we need to do in life. We can confront the past and face the future boldly. We don't have what it takes in ourselves to be victorious, but we do have God and He is always more than enough. Make an effort to maintain a conscious awareness of God's presence. Say out loud several times a day, "God is with me right now." A lot of our problems with fear are due to us not truly believing that God is with us. We would like some kind of proof that He is with us, but He challenges us to simply believe that He is. He said that without faith we cannot please Him, and that those who would come to Him, *must believe that He is*, and that He is the Rewarder of those who diligently seek Him (see Hebrews 11:6). We should not look to our feelings or circumstances for the proof of God's existence, but we must look to the promises in His Word.

We believe with our heart, and my heart tells me that God is with me. I choose to believe it . . . I want to believe it. I don't want to live in fear, so I choose to believe even without feelings that God is indeed with me. Are you willing to do that? The world demands proof before it will believe, but God is only pleased with faith. Be a man or woman of faith; believe with all your heart that God is with you and will never leave you. Let the words, "God is with me," soak into your consciousness until they become so real to you that you are energized to push past all your fears. Meditate on those words, speak them out loud, and let them become a vital part of your conscious awareness at all times. Remember to stop what you are doing several times a day and say, "God is with me."

Anytime you feel fear say, "I will not fear because God is with me." By speaking out against it, you defuse the power of fear and render it ineffective against you. Satan is a predator, and to a predator fear is a sign of weakness. Don't give him the satisfaction of thinking he has any influence over you. When you confront fear, you will discover strength that you never knew you had.

I was recently watching a television program about a family who moved to Africa to start a game preserve. A little girl and her dad had gone for a walk, and she had wandered away from him. Quite unexpectedly she saw a lion that was slowly moving toward her. When her father saw her and realized what was happening, he quietly came up behind her and told her over and over again, "Stand still and don't run." Though he had his gun loaded and ready in case he needed to intervene, the father explained to his daughter that as long as the lion didn't sense fear in her, he would not view her as prey.

If you're confronted by an enemy or an obstacle that is causing you to be afraid today, listen carefully. That voice you hear in your heart is the voice of your heavenly Father, standing with you and saying, *"Stand still and don't run; you are not prey for the enemy. Fear not, for I am with you."*

CHAPTER 2

Right and Wrong Fear

The reverent and worshipful fear of the Lord is the beginning and the principal and choice part of knowledge...

Proverbs 1:7

This book is dedicated to understanding and overcoming wrong fears, but it is important for us to take a moment to realize that there is one right fear that we should have, and that is the reverential fear of God.

> *There is one right fear that we should have, and that is the reverential fear of God.*

This type of fear is not a tormenting fear that comes from an evil source, and it is not a fear of harm or punishment—it is a type of fear that is good and is a blessing to us. In fact, if we have the proper fear of God, it will eliminate most other fears. Having the fear of God certainly doesn't mean that we should be afraid of God, but instead it refers to a respectful, reverential fear that causes us to be promptly and completely obedient to Him and His ways.

The fear of the Lord is the beginning of all proper knowledge and wisdom.

The reverent and worshipful fear of the Lord is the beginning and the principal and choice part of knowledge [its starting

*point and its essence]; but fools despise skillful and godly
Wisdom, instruction, and discipline.*

Proverbs 1:7

A person actually has no truly valuable knowledge until they
know God deeply and intimately. When they really know Him,
and how wonderful and amazing He is, they will have a respectful and reverential fear of Him. People may have education, but
that does not mean they have wisdom and knowledge that is beneficial to them. The fear of God leads to a life of rest, peace, blessing, and contentment.

*The reverent, worshipful fear of the Lord leads to life, and he
who has it rests satisfied; he cannot be visited with [actual] evil.*

Proverbs 19:23

This doesn't mean that a man will have a trouble-free life, but
it does mean that no matter what happens it will turn around for
good as he continues to reverence and worship God. The man
who has reverential fear, awe, and respect for God can expect to
receive divine help when he needs it.

*The Angel of the Lord encamps around those who fear Him
[who revere and worship Him with awe] and each of them
He delivers.*

Psalm 34:7

It is not easy to explain this type of right fear, and the best way
I know to try is to give these examples:

Suppose you are in a room at work with friends and you are all
laughing, joking, and making lots of noise when your employer

walks in. What will your response be? If you have respect and reverential fear for him, you will quiet down and look to him for approval or disapproval of your actions. You know that he has the power to promote you or take your job from you, and because of that you have a reverential fear of him. This is wisdom and not a bad thing at all. You simply want to please your employer because you don't want to lose your job.

Or, as another example, let's imagine a large group of reporters is waiting for the president of the United States to arrive for a press conference. The room is buzzing with conversation, but the moment the president is announced, everyone rises to stand on their feet, and it is either perfectly quiet or else the room erupts with applause. They would not even consider ignoring him and continuing on with their conversation while remaining seated. Why? Because they have a reverential fear of him. He has great authority and they want to please him.

The tiny bit of reverential fear that people feel in situations like these is minute compared to what we should feel as we realize that we live in God's presence at all times. I am not suggesting that we should be afraid that God will punish us for every little mistake we make, or banish us from His presence if we do something wrong, but we should respect God above all else and seek to please Him in all things. Living with reverential fear of the Lord is more about a heart attitude than anything else. God is not vindictive and anxious to take away our blessings, but we can certainly hinder the flow of them if we don't respect God enough to believe what He has said in His Word about our behavior. When we believe what God says and we follow through with corresponding actions, we are showing Him respect, and that type of respect is called the fear of the Lord.

Without reverential fear we do many foolish things, thinking we can do them with no consequences. God's Word teaches us that He chastises us for our own good because He loves us (see Hebrews 12:5–6). I know a woman who—although she believes in Jesus and would consider herself a Christian—lives with her boyfriend. That means she is regularly committing adultery. I care about this woman, and I am sincerely praying for her because she is hurting herself as well as the heart of God by her actions. I know God is trying to get her attention, but presently she merely makes excuses for her behavior: "Everyone does it." "God understands." "I had a bad marriage, and I am afraid to get into that kind of commitment again." Our excuses don't really excuse us in God's sight! I am concerned that eventually, if she doesn't listen, she will need some severe chastisement from God. God would rather we listen to His Word, but He does love us enough to touch our circumstances if He has to. I wanted my children to obey me when I told them to, but if they persisted in disobedience, I took away their privileges. If you are a parent, I am sure that you do the same thing, so why do we expect any less from God Who is our Father?

We can eliminate God's protection from our lives by disobedience, but the fear of the Lord provides security and a place of safety for us (see Proverbs 14:26). In other words, following God's advice will keep us safe and secure even in tumultuous times.

In my opinion there is not enough teaching or writing about the fear of the Lord, and I think it must be because teachers and writers are trying to be careful not to put a wrong fear into the hearts and minds of people. I don't want people to be afraid of God, but I do want them to have a reverential fear of Him. Without it, people find it easy to disobey, and disobedience always leads to a guilty conscience, a loss of fellowship with God, and an open door for the devil. If we'll quickly repent and receive

God's forgiveness when we disobey Him, none of that happens. However, if we think that we can willfully and knowingly ignore God's instructions and still experience the full blessings of God, we are mistaken.

To be honest, I am reverently afraid to knowingly disobey God. It is a fear that is born out of love for Him. We love Him and therefore we want to please Him in all things. I am not afraid of losing my salvation, or even of God being angry with me, but my experience with God has taught me that He is always right in what He says. Therefore, if God teaches us to do or not to do a thing, we should immediately assume that He is right and joyfully do as He has commanded. A person with a reverential fear of God will do just that! This doesn't mean that they never make mistakes, but they do strive to be obedient to God. They know that God is holy, just, and always right in all of His ways. It is impossible for any error to be found in Him.

> *If God teaches us to do or not to do a thing, we should immediately assume that He is right and joyfully do as He has commanded.*

> [Live] as children of obedience [to God]; do not conform your-selves to the evil desires [that governed you] in your former igno-rance [when you did not know the requirements of the Gospel].
>
> But as the One Who called you is holy; you yourselves also be holy in all your conduct and manner of living.
>
> 1 Peter 1:14–15

It is good to feel comfortable in God's presence and to believe that He is not only a loving, forgiving Father, but also your friend; however, that view of God, although it is totally correct, can cause problems if it is not balanced with a healthy, reverential fear of Him also. As a Bible teacher, I have observed how excited people are to hear about the love and mercy of God, and how their enthusiasm diminishes when I speak of the reverential fear of the Lord. We should be thrilled to hear about both because we need both to maintain a wholesome walk with God.

Being a victorious child of God, who is successful in life, is quite easy once we have this loving, reverential fear and decide to promptly obey God. Consider this Scripture:

> ...*What eye has not seen and ear has not heard and has not entered into the heart of man, [all that] God has prepared (made and keeps ready) for those who love Him [who hold Him in affectionate reverence, promptly obeying Him and gratefully recognizing the benefits He has bestowed].*
>
> 1 Corinthians 2:9

It appears to me that God is looking for those with reverential fear to pour outrageous blessings on because those are the people He knows He can trust.

Reverential Fear and Sin

> *The reverent fear and worshipful awe of the Lord [includes] the hatred of evil; pride, arrogance, the evil way, and perverted and twisted speech I hate.*
>
> Proverbs 8:13

This Scripture tells us that the reverent fear of the Lord will cause us to hate evil and all of its ways. Do you hate evil and wickedness? Not just that of others, but your own? You should, and so should I. We should not hate ourselves because we sometimes do evil things, but we should be very quick to repent, and we should hate the evil thing because we know that it displeases God. Actually, we find that the more we hate evil, the less of it we will do. Perhaps our attitude toward evil is too loose and flimsy. We are not to hate evil people, but we should despise the evil deeds they do. We are called by God to love sinners but not to adopt their ways. The apostle Paul encouraged the Ephesians to live carefully, and I think that is good advice. We should be careful about our thoughts, words, attitudes, and actions, knowing that God is all-powerful, all-knowing, and He is everywhere all the time. God sees everything and nothing is hidden from Him.

God is certainly merciful, and we are regularly forgiven for sins and misdeeds, but that does not mean that we should live loosely and without caution, compromising frequently. If we do, then we do not have the fear of the Lord.

Let's consider sexual immorality as an example. It is rampant in the world today, and the church has not been exempt. Statistics on how many people regularly view pornography are shocking. Fornication and adultery are widespread, and sadly they are often accepted by much of society as a "more modern lifestyle."

Large portions of Proverbs are devoted to telling people what the consequences of sexual immorality will be, but people continue to let their passions rule them instead of having the fear of the Lord. I am deeply concerned and pray daily that those of us who know God's Word won't compromise our values, but that we will be a good example for others to follow.

I have seen untold misery and agony in the lives of people simply because family members got involved in sexual immorality. I recently met a woman who stopped me on the street because she recognized me from my television program. She was one of the most miserable people I have met in a long time. She told me that her husband was a minister and she had discovered that he had been having affairs with other women for many years. He was continuing in ministry during this time and living a totally deceptive life. She had become so bitter that she started having affairs herself and was currently involved with another man. She asked for my advice, and when I told her to repent and get out of the immoral relationships, she told me that she knew it was terribly wrong but didn't think she wanted to give it up! I prayed with her that she would decide to do the right thing but will admit that I walked away astonished! She knew what was making her miserable. She knew it was her bitterness, unforgiveness, and her own immoral behavior, and yet she wasn't willing to give it up? It would seem that neither she nor her husband currently have a proper fear of the Lord. Making a mistake is one thing, but living in sin purposely and thinking it is not a problem is another thing entirely!

We speak often of God's grace, forgiveness, and mercy, and they are wonderful! But they should make us love God all the more and urge us to live better lives, not lives filled with undisciplined and ungodly behavior. I do believe that a proper fear of God would prevent a lot of sin. And, in my personal opinion, we need more teaching on this subject. Any subject in God's Word that is ignored in the pulpit is usually ignored in people's lives.

> *And Moses said to the people, Fear not; for God has come to prove you, so that the [reverential] fear of Him may be before you, that you may not sin.*
>
> Exodus 20:20

In this Scripture we see the word "fear" used two times in two different ways. Moses told the people not to have a wrong fear, but he also urged them to have a reverential fear of the Lord. He also states that the right kind of fear will prevent them from sinning.

Respect and Honor

The early church that we read about in the book of Acts regularly experienced amazing miracles. God's power moved among them in an unprecedented way, but the church was also full of respect, honor, and submission, not only to the authority of God, but also to one another.

> *And a sense of awe (reverential fear) came upon every soul, and many wonders and signs were performed through the apostles...*
>
> Acts 2:43

People frequently ask, "Where are the miracles today that existed in the early church?" Perhaps we should ask, "Where is the reverential fear of the Lord that existed in the early church?" Miracles and a reverential fear of the Lord go hand in hand—we won't have one without the other.

The media today often make fun of God, and they are disrespectful toward Him, even to the point of having the audacity to suggest that He be set aside so that those who don't choose to believe in Him won't feel uncomfortable!! How totally ridiculous our society has become. The results of having such an attitude are evident in the world we now live in. We would see an outpouring of God's blessings and power in the world if we would also see a return to respecting, honoring, and being submissive to Him. The fear of the Lord is a beautiful and wise thing, and although there are many fears that we want to avoid and resist, the reverential fear of God should be embraced and sought after ardently.

CHAPTER 3

The Source of Fear

For the Spirit God gave us does not make us timid, but gives us power, love and self-discipline.

2 Timothy 1:7 (NIV)

We can readily see from this one Scripture verse that God is not the source of fear. Although people don't usually enjoy hearing of or learning about Satan, it is impossible to locate the source of fear without talking about him, because he is the source of all wrongful fear. We do have an enemy, and one who is constantly on the prowl, looking for opportunities to kill, steal, and destroy (see John 10:10). We are expected to resist him.

> *So be subject to God. Resist the devil [stand firm against him], and he will flee from you.*
>
> James 4:7

All of Satan's works are done under the cover of deceit, often making it difficult to detect his work. He even camouflages himself at times as an angel of light. Satan is even willing to quote Scripture to us, but it will always be used in a wrong context when he does.

For example, if the devil is trying to get us to do something unwise and foolish, we might hear in our thoughts, *Have faith in*

God. However, the wise and well-informed believer knows the difference between real faith and foolishness and presumption. When we step out in faith to do something that perhaps frightens us, we must be sure that it is God's Word we are stepping out on and nothing else. Peter stepped out of the boat and attempted to walk on water, but he had a definite word of the Lord to do so. I am sure he felt some caution and concern (healthy fear), but at the word of the Lord, he was willing to "do it afraid." That is entirely different from what it would be for me to jump off a diving board into the deep end of a swimming pool when I am a very poor swimmer and would be very afraid to do it. If I thought, *Have faith in God and jump*, I could be assured it was Satan trying to drown me.

Here we must learn the difference between a holy, healthy fear and a tormenting, self-defeating fear. God will give us wisdom and holy caution, and it should be adhered to, but Satan will give us tormenting fear that prevents us from moving forward in obedience to God and doing His will.

Every Believer Has Authority over Satan

We need to recognize and accept that we have an enemy who seeks to destroy and torment us, but we need not be afraid of him. The truth is that as believers in Jesus Christ, we have authority over him, and all we need to do is learn to exercise it.

> *Behold, I give unto you power to tread on serpents and scorpions, and over all the power of the enemy: and nothing shall by any means hurt you.*
>
> Luke 10:19 (KJV)

Satan does indeed have power, but he has no authority to use it against God's children unless they allow him to. He may come against us, but he will not be ultimately successful in executing his evil plans if we resist him, while also maintaining an intimate relationship with God. Actually, Jesus already defeated him when He died on the cross. The purpose for which Christ came was to destroy the works of the devil (see 1 John 3:8). Jesus was successful, so how can Satan still cause trouble if he has been defeated? Jesus destroyed Satan's right to do his evil work, but it is our responsibility to use the authority that God gave us and keep him in his place.

> Jesus destroyed Satan's right to do his evil work, but it is our responsibility to use the authority that God gave us and keep him in his place.

We have spiritual weapons to use against Satan, but they are of no value unless we do use them. The name of Jesus and the authority it holds has been given to us, as well as the Word of God, which is referred to as the sword of the Spirit (see Ephesians 6:17). We can and must use both of them in prayer and confession. We also have the cross of Jesus Christ and His shed blood as powerful weapons. We should remember them when we are under attack, and remember that even the mention of them drives the enemy backward.

Don't view yourself as a helpless victim, but as a powerful and authoritative child of God who does not travel through life alone, but with Jesus Who is Himself a mighty warrior and the Captain of the Host of God's army of angels.

We are taught in God's Word to give no place to the devil (see Ephesians 4:27). We can do this in a variety of ways, but we can also avoid doing it by obedience to God's Word. We do not have to live in fear of Satan because he is a defeated foe—all we need to do is remember that and be more aggressive against him than he is against us.

The Work of Satan in the Human Mind

One of Satan's devices that we must recognize so we can resist and overcome him is his evil work in the human mind.

> *For the weapons of our warfare are not of the flesh, but mighty before God to the casting down of strongholds; casting down imaginations, and every high thing that is exalted against the knowledge of God and bringing every thought into captivity to the obedience of Christ.*
>
> 2 Corinthians 10:4–5 (ASV)

Satan desires to control man's thoughts, because he well knows that man's thoughts determine his actions. He injects thoughts in the mind of man, hoping man accepts them as his own and acts accordingly. Our goal should be to know God's Word well enough to immediately reject all thoughts that don't agree with God and replace them with our own thoughts chosen from God's Word.

Fearful thoughts are among his favorite to use in trying to deceive and diminish God's children. God has a large, free, and full life planned for us, but Satan seeks to diminish us in every possible way. He is a thief and a liar.

We should immediately investigate the source of any thought or imagination that causes us to shrink back or be diminished. Fear always steals from us. It torments us, preventing progress and growth in our lives. God is definitely not the source of any such thought or imaginings, but Satan is!

If we would keep our mind engaged on positive things and not let it be idle and passive, Satan would have no opportunity. We can think our own thoughts instead of merely waiting to see what thoughts are forced on us. Learn to recognize thoughts that are unclean, slanderous, and divisive as well as fearful, and reject them immediately. I have heard it said that you cannot prevent a bird from flying over your head, but you certainly can refuse to let it make a nest in your hair. We might say the same thing of Satan's desire to control our thoughts. We cannot keep him from trying to use our minds for his evil work, but we can prevent his success.

Here is a partial list of fear-based thoughts that we should resist:

If you try to do that, you will fail.
That is not going to work, so don't even try.
What will people think of you if you do that?
You'd better just play it safe. It is better to be safe than sorry.
Don't even try because it will take too much effort.
This is going to be too hard.
Nobody has ever done this before, so what makes you think
    that you can?
You are going to end up lonely.
Nobody loves you.
You will never have enough money.

…and on and on the list could go. But thankfully we can educate ourselves concerning the nature, will, and purpose of God for our lives, and we can resist the devil because he has no authority over us except what we give him through deception or inactivity.

The Work of Satan on Man's Body

Many believers have a great deal of pain, sickness, and weakness in their physical bodies and are prevented from doing the things they want to do because of them.

Many sicknesses are indeed real physical ailments that will need medical attention, but some are lying-symptoms that Satan presents to us in the hope that we will take them as our own. This kind of sickness will disappear if you will resist it immediately.

Right now lots of people have colds. A few days ago it was late in the evening and my throat was feeling sore. The thought came to me, "Oh no, I am getting sick, and I am getting ready to leave town and will probably be sick on the entire trip!" Thankfully, I have some experience with Satan's tactics, so I immediately prayed for healing and then I confessed out loud that I was resisting the symptoms of sickness and that I believed that God's healing power was working in me. I did not get sick! The Bible teaches us to resist the devil at his onset because he roams about as a lion, roaring in fierce hunger, seeking whom he may devour (1 Peter 5:8–9). When you feel symptoms of sickness, pray and resist them immediately. Don't ever wait to see what happens or what disease you might be catching or coming down with before you pray.

I will also admit that there have been other times when I have had symptoms and done the same thing and did indeed get sick. In those instances I was not dealing with a lying-symptom from Satan but a true illness that needed attention. I suggest that you don't accept any sickness without questioning its validity. Satan will give us anything that we are willing to accept, but it is amazing how much misery we can avoid by the simple act of resistance. Even if you remain sick after resisting, I recommend that you continue to pray and don't in any way cooperate with the sickness. Even when you take medicine, pray that God will make it work in your body and that you will have a speedy recovery.

Satan will attack us with tiredness and then put thoughts in our mind that we are not able to finish the task we are involved in. Many times I have felt this way and have stopped and simply asked God to strengthen me, and my energy returned as I continued on with the project. My energy may not have returned immediately, but as I continued in faith I was indeed energized. Don't give up without a fight! Stand your ground, resist the devil, and he will flee.

Because of my extensive travels and work for the Lord, it is a high priority for me to maintain good health and high energy levels. I use wisdom by eating healthy foods, getting proper sleep and rest, and exercising on a regular basis. I trust God to keep me strong to do His work. There have been numerous times over the years when I have felt so bad that I seriously wondered if I would be able to go to the pulpit and deliver my message. Thoughts of weakness, defeat, and failure pounded my mind, but I have yet to have God fail to strengthen me when the time came for me to speak. I could have let the symptoms rule, but I concluded that if God did send me, then surely He wanted me to finish what I started. I merely kept putting one foot in front of the other, and by doing that, many times I have experienced the symptoms leaving. My point is that I didn't just let the symptoms rule me without at least making an effort in the Holy Spirit to resist and overcome them.

Timid and fearful people are easily defeated by even minor physical symptoms, but bold and courageous people will confront and press through if at all possible.

The Work of Satan in the Conscience

Satan attacks the conscience with the fear that we have sinned and that God is displeased with us or even angry with us. Although our conscience is designed to approve or disapprove of our actions, and it does let us know when we have done something wrong, it does not teach us through fear. The Holy Spirit will lead us into all truth and make us aware of our wrong actions so we may repent and start fresh, but He absolutely will never press us down with a burden of fear regarding our actions. Satan, however, will pressure us, threaten us, and present to our mind and emotions and conscience many fearful thoughts about our sin.

God has taken care of the problem of sin, and all any believer needs to do upon being made aware of his sin is to repent, let go of what lies behind him, and press toward the future in faith.

> The fear of sin will hold us in sinful behavior, while focusing on Jesus will lift us out of it.

The fear of sin will hold us in sinful behavior, while focusing on Jesus will lift us out of it. Jesus did not save us so we could remain in bondage to fear (Romans 8:15). To be honest, sin is not a problem for God, because He has already provided the answer in Jesus Christ. Sin becomes a problem only when we let it rule us, or when we remain guilty and fearful instead of receiving the free gift of God's forgiveness. What separates us from God is not sin that we have repented of, but a guilty conscience. Satan knows this and he works very hard to make us feel afraid that we have sinned more times than God is willing to forgive us for. Truthfully, you can come boldly to the throne of God and receive the grace you need to restore you at any time and as many times as you need to.

In Whom, because of our faith in Him, we dare to have the boldness (courage and confidence) of free access (an unreserved approach to God with freedom and without fear).

Ephesians 3:12

The Work of Satan for the Purpose of Torment

Many of the fears and phobias that people experience are designed for no other reason than to torment people. Satan is dedicated to making people miserable, and filling them with fear is one of the best ways to do so. Fear is a sickening, weakening, and defeating feeling. Franklin Roosevelt said that the only thing we have to fear is fear itself, and I totally agree. Once we let fear integrate its roots into our thoughts, emotions, conscience, and actions, we can be assured of torment.

Every human being wants to be free. We want to try new things, and we have a desire for adventure. We are created by God to have goals and press toward them, and to dream of bigger and better things than what we have. Fear leaves us frozen in place, unable to do much of anything except be idle and alone with our torment.

Please be assured that Jesus died not only for the forgiveness of your sins, but also to assure that you might enjoy a fruitful and powerful life. Be determined to have all that He died to give you.

We will talk about phobias later in the book, and you will find the list of them to be astonishing. Many of them make no sense at all, and you will think, "Why would someone be afraid of that?" People with phobias of all kinds usually either simply put up with the phobia, or they repeatedly try to deal with the problem without ever getting to the root of it, which is Satan. If these people only knew to resist the devil, they could experience freedom.

Satan's purpose is merely to torment them and keep them so busy fighting with their symptoms that they have no time or energy to simply live life and enjoy it.

Satan wants our joy because it is our strength (see Nehemiah 8:10). He attacks with fear in order to steal the joy that Jesus has provided for us. He also uses the same tactic to steal our peace. Fear leaves us worried and anxious and can even produce illness if it is permitted to linger for long periods of time. Most fearful people are also unhealthy people. They have many weaknesses like weak stomachs, weak backs, weak determination, and weak minds. They are easily upset emotionally and enjoy very few emotionally stable days.

Whether you have been a fearful person or not, I am hopeful that making you aware of how Satan works will energize you to resist him like never before. God's Word instructs us to "watch and pray," and it is good advice. Watch your thoughts, pay attention to what your emotions are doing, how you're feeling, and what decisions you are making. If you are sensing the beginning of anything that seems the least bit ungodly or that will diminish you in any way, pray immediately and resist in the power of God.

Fear is not from God, but it is from Satan and it is designed to prevent, diminish, and torment. I often say that "fear is the master spirit that Satan uses to do his dirty work." Watch out for fear and face it with boldness and confidence in God.

Don't Let Fear Make You Ineffective

We all have a deep desire to be needed, useful, and productive, and to have a good effect on the lives of other people and the world we live in. This is a godly desire and should be pursued through faith. Satan of course wants to make us ineffective, and he can be successful if we give in to the spirit of fear. Many times we don't share our faith with others due to fear. At other times we don't participate in something due to the fear of being rejected or failing. Fear holds us back, but faith urges us forward. Faith says, "Step out and try," but fear says, "Don't try because you will make a fool of yourself."

We will feel fear, but we can trample on it and leave it in the dust as we press forward in God. The psalmist David admitted that he felt fear and he said,

> *What time I am afraid, I will have confidence in and put my trust and reliance in You.*

> Psalm 56:3

You can be assured that fear will present itself to you at the start of anything you attempt to do that will benefit you or anyone else. At least it will until you are so well advanced in walking by faith that fear's threats only sound like a faint noise in the background. I can honestly say that I am not hindered by fear very much at this point in my walk with God, but I have to be ever-ready to confront it. People ask me if I feel fear when I stand in front of an auditorium filled with people to speak, and I can honestly say that I don't, but there was a time when I did.

There was a time when I had to make a decision to let fear rule, or to rule fear. Don't let fear make you ineffective. If you do, you will live with many regrets over the things you wish you would have done, but never did. The only way to avoid regret is to take action when an opportunity presents itself. It is better to have tried and failed than not to have tried at all.

Don't accept the lie that you are just a timid person, or that "fearful" is just your personality or the way that you are. Some people may be more naturally bold than others are, but everyone can be effective and do amazing things in their lives if they will walk in faith and follow God. It helps us to resist fear if we are certain that Satan is the source of it. If we believe it is just the way we are, then we will accept it and sink into a low level of living that is not God's will. Godly aggression is the key to effectiveness. We can't even be effective in conquering daily chores if we don't attack them with an aggressive attitude.

Always lean on God and depend on His grace (undeserved favor) to make you victorious in your fight against fear. God is your deliverer! Know that God loves you, that He is for you, and He is always with you, and then go forward and don't look back!

CHAPTER 4

Phobias

Fear makes the wolf bigger than he is.

German proverb

Phobias are the unfortunate result of fear: an exaggerated terror that robs the individual of a normal life. These extreme fears range from the common to the absurd, haunting millions by holding them in their irrational grip. You might say a phobia is fear on steroids.

This section of the book should help us understand the lengths to which Satan will go in order to destroy the quality of life God wants us to enjoy. Phobias are life-destroyers. But let us remember, even the strongest fear is no match for our God. The greatest and strongest fear must cower at the name of Jesus. And to the person being tormented by it, an intense phobia may seem like an overwhelming flood of emotions rushing against them that they cannot control. But there is an answer.

When the enemy shall come in like a flood, the Spirit of the Lord will lift up a standard against him and put him to flight.

Isaiah 59:19

When individuals are being attacked with fear or phobias of any kind, they need not try to fight the battle on their own. They can put their faith in God and trust that He will give them victory. The enemy may come against us one way, but God's Word says that he will flee before us seven ways (see Deuteronomy 28:7). No matter what your battles in life may be, I urge you not to ever try to fight them on your own. God will fight for you if you ask Him to.

Definitions of phobias are abundant. *Merriam-Webster's Dictionary* says they are an exaggerated, usually inexplicable and illogical fear of a particular object, class of objects, or situation.

The Mayo Clinic defines phobias as an overwhelming and unreasonable fear of an object or a situation that poses little real danger.[1]

Unlike a brief anxiety most people feel when they give a speech or take a test, a phobia is long-lasting, causes intense physical and psychological reactions, and can affect your ability to function normally at work or in social settings.

Although definitions are plentiful, they vary somewhat. Most of them do say that the phobias and the behavior they cause are an abnormally fearful response to a danger that is imagined or irrationally exaggerated.

How many phobias are there?

The list of phobias is never ending because it is ever expanding. There are phobias that people deal with today that were unheard of twenty-five years ago, or even just a few years ago. We must understand that Satan is very creative in his methods of torment. Once a new phobia is publicized, we then hear of more and more people being tormented by the same problem. Things that we never heard of are now widespread. For as many situations as you can imagine, there is a phobia for each one. There are hundreds of phobias listed online. The most recent online searches report that there are over 500.

Ten most common phobias:[2]

1. People
   (One quarter of the population reports excessive fears of at least one social situation, with public speaking fears topping the list.)
2. Animals
3. Heights
   (More than 20 percent of adults report having had an irrational fear of heights.)
4. Agoraphobia
   (Typically involves a fear of public places, open spaces, or traveling. When it's severe, people can become housebound—literally trapped by fear.)
5. Claustrophobia
6. Flying
7. Blood/Injury/Infections
8. Water/Drowning
9. Storms (thunder and lightning)
10. Being in a crowd

Ten especially peculiar phobias:[3]

1. Fear of vegetables
2. Fear of tight clothing
3. Fear of buttons
4. Fear of clowns
5. Fear of knees

6. Fear of butterflies
7. Fear of flutes
8. Fear of losing mobile phone connectivity
9. Fear of a specific place
10. Fear of phobias

Here are a few others I have heard of from various sources: The fear of beautiful women, the fear of being touched, the fear of drafts or airborne diseases causing people to wear masks in public, the fear of seeing one's own reflection in glass, fear of constipation, the moon, the sunlight, birds or other flying objects, the fear of sitting down, and of course there are fears of every animal one might imagine. The more of these lists I read, the more angry I become at Satan who is the source of all fear, and the more determined I am to see people find freedom.

I would like to say up front that I don't claim to have the clinical or medical answers to problems such as these phobias present, but I do know some spiritual things that I believe will help. I am not a psychologist or a psychiatrist, but I do know God's Word and have decades of experience in watching it set people free. Many times I have witnessed God's Word and power setting people free from addictions and phobias who had gone through many years of counseling and various treatment programs to no avail. I will offer the help I believe I am qualified to give, and should you need other help, please seek it out. And above all, please do not give up, because God is able and willing to help you. Hope is one of the most powerful forces on Earth. As long as you have hope, the door is open for change.

Hope is one of the most powerful forces on Earth. As long as you have hope, the door is open for change.

Pull the Weed Before It Takes Root

When a seed is planted, it takes a while before it has long and strong roots. Should the seed be dug up and discarded before it has opportunity to take root, there would never be any fruit from it. There are good seeds and bad ones, things we would want to get rooted in our lives and things that we would not want to get rooted. When we experience a thought, an emotion, a behavior, or in this instance, a fear that we don't want to become a permanent fixture, the best thing to do is resist it at its onset. Be aggressive in confronting it and firm in your decision not to give in to it. Always remember that the longer you let something linger, the longer it will take to get rid of it.

If someone makes me angry and I deal with my anger immediately, refusing to let it linger, I am normally able to move past it right away; however, if I hang on to it for a few days, then I find I have a bigger fight on my hands when I want to say good-bye to it.

This theory of resisting at the onset will only be helpful when new fears present themselves. I am sure many of you have ones that are already deeply rooted in your life, but new ones are always trying to gain an entrance. Beware and resist them at the onset. Even if you must resist them several times, do so. Don't ever merely submit to fear without a fight. But when you fight fear, always remember to fight in God's power and not your own.

Be Reasonable

Since phobias are defined as "unreasonable" fears, it may seem odd for me to suggest that we examine them with reason and logic, but I do believe this must be done as part of the freeing process. With God's help, we can attempt to be reasonable about an unreasonable fear. For example: I once heard of a woman who had struggled with being overweight most of her life. She eventually had a child and was so fearful that the child would grow up and be overweight that she began exercising the baby's little arms and legs daily while the baby was still in the crib. A bit of rational common sense would have shown her that exercising the infant's limbs would not in any way affect the child's weight later on in life.

Some disabling fears are the result of a traumatic event that took place sometime in a person's life. The natural tendency is to fear that whatever happened will happen again, so we put up all of our defense mechanisms in order to never have to experience that thing again. Whatever happened caused pain, but fearing it will happen again keeps the pain fresh in our minds. Actually, statistically speaking, if something happens to a person once, like their house being robbed, then they are less likely to ever have it happen again. I know that is merely logic and probably doesn't soothe anyone's emotions, but it is true—and realizing that may help somewhat. We may think that we are protecting ourselves from a reoccurrence of something unpleasant through fear, but we are only tormenting ourselves. And the truth is that fearing it wouldn't prevent it from happening anyway. We would be better off spending our energy praying and trusting God!

The apostle Paul wrote that the mind of the flesh is sense and reason without the Holy Spirit (see Romans 8:6). We are called to live a life of faith, and that often has nothing to do with logic. God leads us from our spirit, not from our head. The person who relies too much on their intellect finds it very difficult to believe in and have an intimate relationship with God. Although sense and reason without the Holy Spirit is not a good idea, I believe that sense and reason (common sense) *with* the Holy Spirit is a very good idea. As we pray about the things in our lives for which we need answers, God will lead and guide us through His Holy Spirit. He often reveals simple and very practical things that we can do to help us in our situation. They are commonsense things that are very logical, and we should follow His advice.

I was shopping one day and purchased a small jar of skin care for my eyes. When I was paying, the clerk asked if I knew I could purchase a second jar for 50 percent off. I did not know that, and I decided it would be a good deal. Then I asked if all the products in that brand were being offered at the same sale price. She said that they were and I immediately (and I might add emotionally) went back to the items and started choosing pairs of several things. Then I took a minute and thought it over. I asked myself, *Do I really need these items? What else do I already have at home in similar products?* Then the thought came to me that other things would be on sale at another time and that I didn't need to spend money just to think I was saving money. I made my original purchase and left. In this instance I was being reasonable and logical (I believe with God's guidance), and it was a good thing.

Shopping is quite different from a tormenting phobia, but the principle is the same. I have learned that God's principles can be applied anywhere we need them. The next time you recognize a fear of any kind tempting you, try talking to yourself about it a little and look at it logically and reasonably. Normally when emotion flares up, all logic disappears, but it doesn't have to.

I recall a day 46 years ago when I spent an afternoon sitting on top of the kitchen table waiting for my husband to get home because I had captured a mouse in the bathroom and was afraid it would get out!! I can tell you that there was no logic that day at all. Had I thought about it reasonably, I could have realized that the mouse (which was a baby) had no way or desire to harm me in the first place. Even if I saw it again, how could it actually hurt me? It had no hands to reach or turn the doorknob on the bathroom door and get out, but I sat on the tabletop (I was eight months pregnant) and waited for Dave to get home. Multitudes of women are terrified of mice, and yet these creatures have no true ability to harm us.

When Dave did come home, he untied the bathroom door (yes, I had it tied to another door with a rope) and he found the mouse under the plunger where I had trapped it. It had suffocated and lay upside down, with all fours in the air. It was a pink baby about two inches long. Fierce, indeed! Ridiculous, to say the least, but that is a good example of what unreasonable fear will do to a person if they leave their emotions unchecked.

We need to be like the 84-year-old grandmother who fiercely maintained her independence and lived alone in the old family home. Her four children lived in the same town, but she rarely called them except in emergencies. It was with some apprehension, therefore, that one of her sons drove to her house one morning in answer to her phone call. When he arrived, she said she suspected that there was a burglar in her bedroom closet, since she had heard noises in there the night before. "Why didn't you call me last night?" "Well," she replied, "it was late and I hated to bother you, so I just nailed the closet shut and went to bed." That's the kind of attitude we can have when faced with fears of all kinds. Nail the door of fear shut and go to bed in calm assurance.[4]

We may perhaps close the door on many fears by being less emotional and applying more sense and reason in the Holy Spirit. Ask yourself, *What can possibly happen if I don't give in to this fear that is demanding unreasonable behavior from me?* Quite often the answer will be, "Nothing will happen."

Lloyd Douglas said, "If a man harbors any sort of fear, it percolates through all his thinking, damages his personality, and makes him landlord to a ghost."[5] In other words, he wastes his time on something that isn't even a reality.

It is reported that 6.3 million Americans have a diagnosed phobia. Just imagine how many suffer with these crippling and unreasonable fears and keep them a secret. Statistics state that 60 percent of the things people fear will never take place, 90 percent of the things feared are considered to be insignificant, and 88 percent of things feared in relation to health will never happen.[6]

I realize it is easier for me to be logical about these phobias because I don't have them. I have empathy for people who suffer with these problems, and I realize that the symptoms they have can seem overwhelming. And although some of the spiritual solutions that I am offering are somewhat simple, we often find that the answers to complicated problems are simple. We look for complicated answers to complicated problems, but the simple truth of God's Word

> *We often find that the answers to complicated problems are simple.*

is that He loves us, and all things are possible with Him. Come to Him in faith like a little child and believe that He can set you free.

A man who is afraid of everything dies a thousand deaths, but the courageous man dies only once. If we truly want to be free from fear, perhaps we could reason that no matter how difficult it would be to do the thing we fear, it wouldn't be as bad as being afraid of it all of our lives.

Do It Afraid

While I was watching a program about people being treated for phobias, I realized that the doctors attending them were trying to find the root of their problem, reason with them and get them to the point where they would do what they were afraid of in order to get over it. I thought how amazing it was that these people had spent thousands and thousands of dollars to get advice that God gives us in His Word—free of charge. Don't be afraid to face the real problem behind the phobia. The man who is afraid of beautiful women is actually dealing with a deep-rooted insecurity in himself and a belief that no attractive woman would be interested in him. He is not actually afraid of beautiful women; he is afraid of himself, or afraid that he doesn't meet the standard of what he imagines he should be. The woman I heard about who exercised her infant's tiny arms and legs in an effort to be sure the child never became overweight was actually afraid of her own large body size.

The only way to conquer fear is to confront it and to do the thing you are afraid of. Let me add that it should be something that actually needs to be done. If you are afraid of flying and you never need to fly anywhere, then just forget it. But if your fear of flying is adversely affecting your life, do it afraid and get beyond it. If you're afraid of pigs, then just don't go in a pigpen, but if you're afraid of open spaces, you will need to go out . . . even if you have to do it afraid. If you don't, you will be a prisoner all of your life. When we do confront things, we always find that the worst part of the fear was in our minds, and that the reality of the thing wasn't as bad as we had imagined.

I once heard a story, which I told in my book *The Confident Woman*. It was about a village where the children were told,

"Whatever you do, don't go near the top of the mountain. It's where the monster lives." One day, some brave young men decided they wanted to see the monster and defeat it. Halfway up the mountain, they encountered a huge roar and a terrible stench. Half the men ran down the mountain, screaming. The other half of the men got farther up the mountain and noticed that the monster was smaller than they had expected—but it continued to roar and emit such a stench that all but one man ran away. As he took another step forward, the monster shrank to the size of a man. Another step and it shrank again. It was still hideously ugly and stank, but the man could actually pick it up and hold it in the palm of his hand. He said to the monster, "Who are you?" In a tiny, high-pitched voice, the monster squeaked, "My name is fear."

Just as the monster got smaller and smaller with each step the man took toward it, so our fears will become smaller and smaller the more we confront them.

Thoughts and Fear

Wrong thoughts lead to wrong actions and reactions. If you are dealing with fear in general or some specific fear, I encourage you to examine your thought life and you may quickly find the source of your problem. Fearful thoughts will never produce a fearless life! I had the joy of writing a book many years ago called *Battlefield of the Mind*. It is about the warfare that goes on in our mind that is induced by the devil as he attempts to build strongholds in our thinking that will eventually control our behavior. This book has been used by God to set many people free from irrational fears and other addictive behaviors. It teaches us how to think properly and when we do, improper thoughts find no entrance or place to take root and grow.

I recall one woman who testified that she had dealt unsuccessfully with bulimia for years. This disorder causes a person to eat excessively and then make him- or herself vomit in an effort to not gain weight. If this process is repeated often, it can do tremendous damage to the individual's health. She had been in many treatment programs unsuccessfully, but testified that upon reading *Battlefield of the Mind* she gained insight that she had not previously had. She realized her thoughts were controlling her emotions and knew that only right thinking could help her gain freedom. When she felt the urge to make herself vomit after eating, she took her *Battlefield of the Mind* book to the bathroom with her and read it on her knees in front of the toilet. She shared that the truth she found in the book's message gave her the strength not to give in to the addiction that was stealing her life and health, and she was eventually set completely free.

Anytime you feel afraid, you should change your thinking. You don't have to think on whatever falls into your mind, but you can choose your own thoughts and should do so very carefully. Many people do not realize they can cast down one thought and choose another, but they can, and they must if they ever hope to control their actions. God's Word teaches us that as a man thinks, so does he become (see Proverbs 23:7). Right thinking will lead to right living!

Emotional and Physical Symptoms of Fear

The symptoms of fear, both emotional and physical, that people experience will end up controlling their behavior if they don't recognize them for what they are and confront them. When fear is present, we might experience a variety of symptoms ranging from a mild feeling of nervousness, to anxiety and panic attacks that require a hospital visit. People shake, sweat, their heart may race rapidly, or they may feel weak physically. If their breathing is affected, they may start to hyperventilate, making them feel they are suffocating, and that turns into a panic attack. These symptoms make us want to run from whatever is causing the fear. In fact, part of the definition of fear is to take flight or run away from. In short, fear does bring torment on many different levels.

Most people experience the milder symptoms of fear, and it would be easier for them to decide they are going to "do it afraid" no matter what. For those who experience more serious symptoms, they might need to do what they fear a tiny bit at a time, and each time they see progress it will encourage them

> *The Holy Spirit knows us intimately, and we can trust Him to never move us along any faster than we are able to go.*

to believe that they can do even more the next time. The Holy Spirit knows us intimately, and we can trust Him to never move us along any faster than we are able to go.

During the years I was being healed from the sexual and emotional abuse I endured from my father, I was set free in tiny degrees. As the Holy Spirit led me to confront one issue at a time, I experienced freedom. On some occasions I seemed to get over huge obstacles in one leap of faith, but at other times freedom came so slowly that admittedly it often seemed that I was making no progress at all even though I was. The Word of God speaks often of "walking" in faith, or "walking in love," or "walking in the Spirit." Walking is the slowest mode of travel known to man. Walking requires one step after another and another and another, but eventually we get where we are going if we don't give up along the way. It may take some time, but I encourage you to keep "walking" toward total freedom from fear.

CHAPTER 5

Cultivating Courage

*Let us not lose heart and grow weary and faint in acting
nobly and doing right, for in due time and at the appointed
season we shall reap, if we do not loosen and relax our
courage and faint.*

Galatians 6:9

Before we begin discussing the various types of fear we often have
to confront in life, I think it is important to discuss the answer
to all fear, no matter what type it is. We only overcome fear by
believing that God loves us unconditionally, placing our faith in
Him, trusting that He is with us at all times, and letting that give
us the confidence to be courageous.

Perhaps instead of praying for our fears to go away, we should
pray to be courageous enough to press past them. Satan gives us
fear, but God gives us faith, and anything God gives is always
more powerful than what Satan offers. My point is that even
when fear is present, if faith in God and courage are also present,
those things will defeat fear—every time.

Courage is not something we wait to feel before stepping out on it,
but it is a force we believe we are equipped with because we believe
that God is with us. We should pay more attention to what God has
said to us in His Word than we do the lies of Satan. Courage is what
enables us to look at the things we fear and "do them afraid."

One summer morning as Ray Blankenship was preparing his breakfast, he gazed out the window and saw a small girl being swept along in the rain-flooded drainage ditch beside his Andover, Ohio, home. Blankenship knew that farther downstream, the ditch disappeared with a roar underneath a road and then emptied into the main culvert. Ray dashed out the door and raced along the ditch, trying to get ahead of the foundering child. Then he hurled himself into the deep, churning water. Blankenship surfaced and was able to grab the child's arm. They tumbled end over end. Within about three feet of the yawning culvert, Ray's free hand felt something—possibly a rock—protruding from one bank. He clung desperately, but the tremendous force of the water tried to tear him and the child away. *If I can just hang on until help comes...* he thought. He did better than that. By the time the fire-department rescuers arrived, Blankenship had pulled the girl to safety. Both were treated for shock. On April 12, 1989, Ray Blankenship was awarded the Coast Guard's Silver Lifesaving Medal. The award is fitting, for this selfless person was at even greater risk to himself than most people knew. Ray Blankenship can't swim.[1]

Ray Blankenship would have surely been afraid had he taken time to think about what he was about to do, but courage from within motivated him to do what would have seemed impossible to him had he thought about it. I believe we all have courage, but sadly we think too much about the things that frighten us, and those things prevent us from being our best. We are all capable of great things if we will live courageously.

> We are all capable of great things if we will live courageously.

Courage takes a chance and tries to do something rather than passively sitting by and doing nothing. At times a fine line exists between courage and foolishness, and I certainly am not advocating foolishness, but at times we must at least be willing to take a chance if we are ever going to do anything courageously. I have often been told that I cannot do this thing or that thing, yet I have felt that God wanted me to try, and I did. I have attempted to live my life motivated by what I feel in my heart, not what I am told by others. It has worked well for me and although I have made some mistakes, I have had more successes than failures, and that is what people remember. I am admittedly not overly educated or amazingly creative, but I have cultivated faith in God and have chosen courage as a way of life, and you can do the same thing.

When Peter stepped out of the boat to attempt to walk on water as Jesus was doing, I am sure he felt a mixture of fear and courage, and courage won out. He surely knew that he could end up looking foolish in front of the other disciples, but he took a chance. Peter didn't think about the fact that he could not walk on water, he just got out of the boat and tried. He did indeed walk on water for a short distance and then as he saw and thought about the storm he began to sink (see Matthew 14:28–31). The story is not repeatedly told today so people will remember how Peter sank when he tried; instead, we tell it so we remember he DID walk on water. We can see from this one biblical account that heroism and courage is remembered and celebrated. If you believe you are supposed to do something, go for it! Even if you only partially succeed, you will still be better off than those who didn't even try. The worst thing that can happen is you will fail; but if you don't even try, you have failed already.

If miracles were being sold in cans we would all run to the store and buy as many as we could, and the truth is that miracles do come in "cans" . . . they come as we believe that with God, we can!

God Calls Joshua

Be strong, courageous, and firm; fear not nor be in terror before them, for it is the Lord your God Who goes with you; He will not fail you or forsake you.

Deuteronomy 31:6

When God told Joshua that he was to finish leading the Israelites into the Promised Land after Moses had died, I am sure Joshua felt fearful about the task. God wasn't telling him not to *"feel"* fear, He was telling him to face the fear with courage. We see the phrase "fear not" repeated over and over in the Bible. It doesn't mean not to feel fear, but it does mean not to give in to it when we do feel it.

The Word of God is filled with stories of men and women who did astonishing things by faith, and we are never told that they didn't feel fear. In some instances we are clearly told that they did feel fear. Moses was afraid when God appeared to him in the burning bush, Elijah was afraid of Jezebel, surely Abram felt fear when God told him to leave his home and all of his relatives and go to a place that would only be revealed to him after he was on his journey. Esther spoke of her fear of being killed by the king if God didn't give her favor when she went before him to plead for her people. Surely Daniel felt fear when he walked into the lion's den, but he courageously did it afraid. Whether you are familiar with these Bible stories or not, let me assure you that they are accounts of normal people just like you and me who were prompted by God to face their fears and do amazing things.

Joshua was facing a huge task when God told him to fear not and be courageous. What are you facing right now, or what might you face in the future? Whatever it is, you need not fear it, for God has promised to be with you, just as He promised to be with Joshua. Although we may not be equipped to handle some of the things we confront in life, God is. There is nothing too hard for Him! On more than one occasion, God told Joshua to be strong and courageous and keep going forward. We not only feel fear at the beginning of our journey, but it also shows up unannounced at various intervals along the way. The answer to fear is always the same: "Be strong and courageous, for God is with you."

> *The answer to fear is always the same: "Be strong and courageous, for God is with you."*

The need for courage is the reason we should encourage one another. Fear runs rampant in the earth and seeks to hinder all progress, but God has given us the Holy Spirit to encourage us, and He exhorts us to encourage one another. One right word of encouragement from you at the right time may keep someone else from giving up.

God told Moses, before he died, to encourage Joshua.

> *But Joshua son of Nun, who stands before you, he shall enter there. Encourage him, for he shall cause Israel to inherit it.*
>
> Deuteronomy 1:38

Moses also told the people to encourage Joshua.

> *But charge Joshua, and encourage and strengthen him, for he shall go over before this people and he shall cause them to possess the land which you shall see.*
>
> Deuteronomy 3:28

God knew that fear would attack Joshua and that he would need encouragement all along the way. Are you good at encouraging people? It is a vitally important ministry and one that none of us should ignore. When I stepped out to obey the call of God on my life, I had many who discouraged me, and only three who I can remember who encouraged me. Thankfully, by the grace of God, I was able to confront the many fears that came against me with the courage of God, and you can do the same thing. Even if you have no person on this Earth who is encouraging you, you do have the Holy Spirit, and He will encourage you if you will listen to Him. When all men fail us and we feel terribly alone, God is with us just as He has always been. The apostle Paul said, "At my first trial no one... [even] stood with me, but all forsook me. May it not be charged against them! But the Lord stood by me and strengthened me..." (2 Timothy 4:16–17). Just as the Lord stood by Paul and gave him strength, He will do the same for you.

Equipped for the Task

You can be assured that anything God leads you to do, He will equip you to do it. You may not feel or see the abilities and courage that you need, but they will arrive the moment you need them. In God's economy, we must believe first and we will see later. When we trust God and take the steps of faith He is leading us to take, He never fails to provide what we need.

> For this reason I am telling you, whatever you ask for in prayer, believe (trust and be confident) that it is granted to you, and you will [get it].
>
> Mark 11:24

When do we get what we have asked for? After we believe! Sometimes we must even remain steadfast in believing for a period of time before we see what is already ours by faith.

God called a man named Gideon to deliver His people. In the natural, Gideon was a huge coward and he even referred to himself as the least in his father's house and of the poorest clan. He told God that he was not able to do what God was asking (see Judges 6:15). Gideon was talking based on his mind and emotions, but he should have been listening to God and repeating what He was saying to him. God had already sent an angel who appeared to Gideon, and the angel said, "The Lord is with you, you mighty man of [fearless] courage" (Judges 6:12). I think this is amazing. God didn't call Gideon what he was; He called him what He knew Gideon had the ability to be! Gideon didn't see it yet, so he still referred to himself as if he were a natural man without God. It is good to take some time to ask yourself what you truly believe about yourself. Do you believe that God loves you, and that He is with you right now? Do you believe that you can do anything God asks you to do? Stop looking at what you think you are and start listening to God, who is in your heart, trying to encourage you to be courageous and do great things instead of living in fear and taking a backseat in life.

You can do whatever you need to do in life through Christ who strengthens you (see Philippians 4:13). If you will believe that, then an adventurous future awaits you with unlimited possibilities.

I do many things in my ministry that I am not qualified to do in the natural. What I mean is that I have had no formal training to do them, but God has equipped me. I have preached thousands upon thousands of messages and yet no earthly person has ever taught me how to put a sermon together.

It is exciting when you see yourself doing things that you know you couldn't possibly do unless God was doing them through you. God equips us with His anointing (His power). He gives us supernatural ability, by taking our "natural" and adding His "super." God is looking for people who are available, not necessarily those who are able. Gideon knew that in the natural he was not able, but God equipped him for the task.

> God is looking for people who are available, not necessarily those who are able.

Our equipping comes in various ways. God divinely equips us with gifts that enable us to do His will. The Holy Spirit distributes these gifts (abilities) as He wills and for His purpose. It is useless to be unhappy with the gifts we have been given or, for that matter, not given. Some people spend their life wishing they could do things that they are not gifted to do, while ignoring the things they can do. But let me reiterate that God does definitely equip us to successfully do what He leads us to do. We are not equipped to do according to our own will, but we are equipped to do God's will.

We are also strengthened and equipped for our task through diligent study of God's Word. Taking the time to do this is something that we can and must do if we want to be fully prepared for whatever comes our way. Regular study of God's Word keeps you strong spiritually. God's Word says that the strong spirit of a man will sustain him in bodily pain and trouble (see Proverbs 18:14). If you do what you need to do to stay strong, you will experience more victory.

Every Scripture is God-breathed (given by His inspiration) and profitable for instruction, for reproof and conviction of sin, for correction of error and discipline in obedience, [and] for training in righteousness (in holy living, in conformity to God's will in thought, purpose, and action).

So that the man of God may be complete and proficient,
well fitted and thoroughly equipped for every good work.

2 Timothy 3:16–17

When we have knowledge of God's Word that has been tried and tested in our life, it gives us confidence and courage, and that is what we need to confront the spirit of fear.

Another way that we are equipped for our task in life is through the experiences we have. At times we don't understand why God permits us to go through some of the difficulties that we go through, but He always has a purpose—He can use our difficulties for our ultimate good.

Look at what these Scriptures say about Jesus' experience during His years on Earth:

Although He was a Son, He learned [active, special] obedience through what He suffered.

And, [His completed experience] making Him perfectly [equipped], He became the Author and Source of eternal salvation . . .

Hebrews 5:8–9

The things that Jesus experienced in His humanity equipped Him as a merciful high priest who could sympathize with the weaknesses and needs of all people. Sometimes we must go through things in order to fully understand the difficulties that others experience. I believe that each thing we go through helps equip us for our next challenge. Having experience and going through things also help us live courageously. We learn that we can endure difficulties, and that knowledge helps us not to fear future endeavors.

So far we see that we are: (1) Supernaturally equipped by God for our task. (2) Equipped through knowledge of God's Word. (3) Equipped through the experiences we have in life. Let it suffice to say that you are able to do whatever God leads you to do; God knows it, but you need to know it too. If you doubt yourself, then you are likely not to step out, but to draw back in timidity and fear.

Take Courage

Satan offers us fear, but God offers us courage. Which one will you take?

> *But the people, the men of Israel, took courage and strengthened themselves and again set their battle line in the same place where they formed it the first day.*
>
> Judges 20:22

The men of Israel were in a battle with the Benjamites and the men of Gibeah, and at the end of the first day of battle they had lost 22,000 men. After a solid defeat it is even more difficult to be courageous than it was previously. But the Israelites "took courage and strengthened themselves" and positioned themselves for the next battle the same as the day before. The story goes on to say that the second day they lost 18,000 men. Wow! They were being courageous and they were still losing the battle; however, they did not give up. They continued to seek God and go again to battle, and ultimately they did defeat their enemy. I am excited and encouraged by people who refuse to give up!

The men of Israel had a choice to make after their first defeat. Would they take courage or take fear? Would they believe that with God they wouldn't fail and they could try again, or would they take the easy way out and just give up? It takes courage to keep pressing on when you have already experienced failure, but they did it and ended up victorious. Many people who live unfulfilled lives do so because they let one or two failures defeat them. I like to say that we are not failures just because we fail at something. Nobody is a failure until they quit trying.

> We are not failures just because we fail at something. Nobody is a failure until they quit trying.

The men of Israel succeeded for three reasons: (1) God was on their side. (2) They took courage. (3) They strengthened themselves. How did they strengthen themselves? I can only imagine since I wasn't there, but I think they prayed, remembered God's word to them, encouraged one another, and had a good talk with themselves. Sometimes we have to tell ourselves, *I will not give up, and I will succeed.* You might even have to say it repeatedly until it sinks in to your consciousness.

A previous loss may discourage us, but people can also discourage us at times. They look at us in the natural, or as we are, and sometimes they discourage us because they just don't see what God sees. But God sees beyond what we are right now, and He sees what we can be with His help. Don't take the fear that Satan offers you, because if you do, you are taking a destructive force into your life that weakens and disables you. Take courage and strengthen yourself in the Lord!

Courage Is Contagious

Can we catch courage? At first, no; initially, courage must be chosen, but once we get a taste of what courage feels like and we see the benefits it brings, courage becomes contagious! It may start in one area of our life and then spread to all areas. I think the first truly courageous act I did was to finally decide that with God's help I could overcome my painfully horrible past. I decided to stop being a victim and to stop feeling sorry for myself. Once I made that bold decision, courage began to spread through my entire life. Yes, I still had to choose it each time I needed it, but once I had tasted courage, I couldn't stomach fear anymore. Why would anyone choose to live a weak, timid, impotent life after they have experienced the benefits of courage? Usually they won't. They will go from courage to courage and do great things for the glory and honor of God.

The first time I spoke in front of what I thought was a large gathering of people (about 900), I was very afraid. So afraid, in fact, that fear had squeezed my throat shut, and when I initially tried to speak, only a faint squeak came out of me. But I did take courage and I strengthened myself and tried again and was able to speak. That first time ended up being successful. I saw the benefits of courage, and since then I have spoken in front of as many as half a million people at one time in an open-air crusade in India with no fear at all. At this point in my life I am not hesitant to take advantage of any opportunity that God puts in front of me, because I know for certain that if God calls me to do it, He will equip me also. Am I naturally brave? Not really! I have just let courage become contagious in my life. I am addicted to it at this point, and cannot imagine being tormented by fear day and night as I once was. If you are controlled by fear, or if you feel that you have lost opportunities because of it, the good news is that you too can take courage and start enjoying the new opportunities that God will send your way.

I also believe that other people are encouraged as they see us being courageous. They see the joy we have, the power we walk in, and the victory we experience, and they want the same thing. Of course they will have to choose courage, because it won't just be grafted into them, but we do tend to become like the people we are around. If you want more courage, then spend time with people who are courageous and stop spending excessive time with fearful, defeated people.

> If you want more courage, then spend time with people who are courageous and stop spending excessive time with fearful, defeated people.

After God called Gideon to lead His people into victory, and Gideon had finally worked through his own fears and accepted the challenge, the time came when he had to separate himself from other fearful men in order to win the battle.

> *So now proclaim in the ears of the men, saying, Whoever is fearful and trembling, let him turn back and depart from Mount Gilead. And 22,000 of the men returned, but 10,000 remained.*
>
> Judges 7:3

These numbers give us some insight into how many fearful people there are compared to those with courage. Gideon was going to be more powerful with a few courageous men than with a lot of men, most of whom were fearful. Understanding this Scripture has helped me in my own ministry to understand that no matter how fond I am of someone, or how much I don't want to hurt their feelings, I simply cannot do all that God wants me to do with fearful people by my side.

I am willing to work with those who are fearful to help them overcome their fears, but if they persist in being excessively timid, I have to put them in a position where courage is not needed.

For example, when I leave for a trip to a third-world country that has a history of being dangerous, I use God's wisdom and have no fear of going. But the team I take with me must also be courageous. I cannot afford to go into spiritually volatile places with fear. If I did, the devil would recognize my fear and it would open a door for him. We must maintain a high level of confidence all the way through a project if we plan to be successful.

Even if you have suffered setbacks, don't let them fill you with fear. Shake off the disappointment and get reappointed for victory!

CHAPTER 6

Insecurity

*And you shall be secure and feel confident because there is
hope; yes, you shall search about you, and you shall take
your rest in safety.*
    You shall lie down, and none shall make you afraid…
Job 11:18–19

I've read that insecurity is defined as a feeling of general unease
or nervousness that may be triggered by perceiving oneself to be
vulnerable in some way, or a sense of instability that threatens
one's self-image. It is a feeling or belief that we are not acceptable
and that we are not what we ought to be. It is a fear that we will
fail at an important time and everyone will discover that we have
no value. Some people are a little insecure and perhaps only in
one or two areas, but other people are almost crippled with insecurity and it shows up in everything they try to do.

Nearly every person in this world suffers from some form of
insecurity. Whether it's physical, emotional, or spiritual, insecurity is rampant. We might even say that we have an epidemic of
insecure people in society today. In reality there is only one true
form of permanent security, and His name is Jesus. He is the only
one who never changes and He is the only one we can depend on
to be present when we need Him. We can be secure in Him and
His unconditional love for us.

In this section I will quote several Scriptures, and I suggest that you don't skip over them. I am including them because I truly believe that God's Word has power that will comfort us and set us free from fear and insecurity.

> *Let the beloved of the Lord rest secure in him, for he shields him all day long, and the one the Lord loves rests between his shoulders.*
>
> Deuteronomy 33:12 (NIV)

You are the beloved of the Lord! You will have to choose to believe that before any true progress can be made toward enjoying a fearless and secure life. The unconditional love of God is the cure for everything that ails us. It heals broken hearts and souls that are wounded from past abuse. It sets us free from comparison and com-

> *The unconditional love of God is the cure for everything that ails us.*

petition, and it gives us the confidence to be the person that God created us to be. Only in the love of God can we find true security.

Everyone wants to be loved unconditionally. They want to be loved for who they are and not merely for what they do. I will admit that in the world it is difficult (but not impossible) to find that kind of pure, unselfish love, but we can find it abundantly and freely in Jesus. It is referred to as "perfect" love.

> *There is no fear in love [dread does not exist], but full-grown (complete, perfect) love turns fear out of doors and expels every trace of terror! For fear brings with it the thought of punishment, and [so] he who is afraid has not reached the full maturity of love [is not yet grown into love's complete perfection].*
>
> 1 John 4:18

People who are insecure have great difficulty fully believing that God can love them perfectly, completely, and forever. That is because they feel undeserving of love in their imperfect state, and they have not yet learned that God's love is a gift of His grace and not something they can earn or deserve.

How can we believe it? I believe a lot of things about God's promises because I want to. I choose to because believing is what produces peace and joy in my life. I lived many years filled with doubt and unbelief, waiting for some kind of proof that God and His promises were real, and it only produced fear and misery. You can also wait for some proof, which you may never get, or you can accept God's love by faith and begin your journey of wholeness. The faith I have in my heart has become more real to me than any circumstance ever could. Circumstances can quickly and frequently change. If I based God's love on circumstance, one day it appears He loves me and then the next it may seem He doesn't. But when I receive it by faith, it is always mine and can never be taken away from me unless I decide to let it go. This might sound overly simplified, but I believe that we can choose to believe what we want to believe, so why not believe something that will benefit you?

Believe that God loves you. Set your mind and keep it set on the fact that God loves you, not because you deserve it, but because He is love and loving us is simply what He does. There is never a moment in your life when God doesn't love you! He might be displeased with our behavior at times, but His love for us is constant and uninterrupted.

Take all the time you need to bask in the love of God. Jesus said, "Abide in My love" (see John 15:10), and that means live, dwell, and remain in it at all times. Don't let anything separate you from the love of God. The apostle Paul teaches us to get rooted and grounded in the love of God.

> May Christ through your faith [actually] dwell (settle down, abide, make His permanent home) in your hearts! May you be rooted deep in love and founded securely on love.
>
> Ephesians 3:17

Yes, it is only the unconditional love of God that destroys our insecurity and makes us feel secure in Him. Do you have deep roots in the love of God? Roots deep enough to take you through every storm in life without ever wondering whether or not God loves you? I pray that you do, but if you don't, you can get very excited because God is working in your life right now, and He is never going to let you go! God is renewing your mind as you read this book, and I believe it is going to help you freely receive God's love in a greater measure than ever before. With God's help we are never stuck anywhere with no way out. No matter how long you may have suffered with insecurity, God's healing and deliverance is available for you. You are on your way to freedom!

Where Does Insecurity Come From?

I don't believe that we are born insecure, but it doesn't seem to take very long for insecurity to rear its ugly head. What happens? All it takes are a few sad experiences of being made to feel that there is something wrong with us and the seeds of tormenting insecurity are sown.

A young girl has acne on her face, but her best friend has beautiful, clear skin. A young boy is hefty and very tall; he towers over all of his skinny, average-height friends. A nine-year-old girl feels that it is her fault that Mom and Dad got a divorce. A boy with a learning disability doesn't do well in school and he is accused of not reaching his potential simply because everyone has failed to recognize the real problem. A young boy stutters terribly and other children who can often be cruel make fun of him. A woman is married to the man of her dreams and she is devoted to him. She discovers he has been having an affair with another woman, and he leaves her with their two children to care for by herself. A man has worked for a company for 20 years, then without warning he is let go and finds himself unemployed and unable to find a job.

Insecurity can come from any of these types of things and thousands of other things. Satan, the author of fear, is also the author of insecurity, which is in reality a fear that we are not acceptable and that we won't be taken care of.

Although it is good to get to the root of our insecurities to help us understand them better, it is not vital in recovering from them. Some people are extremely insecure and they have no idea why. They had great parents, a good school experience, lots of friends, earned good grades, and had many other pleasant experiences, but secretly they suffer terribly with feelings of inferiority. A person may even live a double life. She appears to be happy to those around her, but in her secret life she has an eating disorder, hates herself, and always feels insecure. The happy face she puts on is a mask that she wears, and she has everyone fooled but herself and the God who created her. Unless these types of problems are confronted, they may develop into more serious anxiety disorders.

Satan's goal is to make us dissatisfied with ourselves and then drive us to unhealthy comparisons with other people. He wants us to waste our lives trying to change ourselves into someone else rather than embrace the amazing person God intends us to be. Resist him at the onset of insecurity! If you have believed all kinds of negative things about yourself and suffered with insecurity, why not say good-bye to insecurity and begin your journey toward safe, confident, and secure living right now. Make a bold declaration out of your mouth and say, *"I resist insecurity. I resist the devil who is the root of insecurity and fear, and I submit myself to God's unconditional love and healing."* By faith, receive the free grace of God that is His undeserved favor and power to change.

> *But He gives us more and more grace (power of the Holy Spirit, to meet this evil tendency and all others fully).*
>
> James 4:6

Grace is always available for us in any situation that we encounter in life. It will lift us up and enable us to be successful in all that we need to do. Please believe that you do not have to continue suffering with insecurity. You can be the bold, courageous person that God intends you to be.

Symptoms of Insecurity

In addition to being fearful, some of the symptoms of insecurity are defensiveness, being overly competitive, materialistic, self-promoting, manipulative, controlling and bullying, jealousy and excessive joking, just to mention a few.

Insecure people tend to be very sensitive to any kind of critique, and their first impulse is to defend themselves and try to convince others that they are unflawed.

They may talk excessively about themselves and what they are doing and accomplishing in an effort to prove that they have value.

They may feel threatened by others, and especially those who are secure, so they attempt to stay in control of every situation. In a desperate effort to appear powerful, they bully, manipulate, and control.

An insecure person may seek to own a lot of things because it makes them feel important. They are often very competitive. Their goal is to be number one in all things because it makes them feel better than other people. But their behavior only showcases their insecurities rather than hiding them as they had hoped. They work so hard at convincing people they are valuable that it wears them out mentally, emotionally, and physically. I know this is true because I was once very insecure, and although I didn't realize it at the time, I was constantly working and trying to prove to myself and everyone else that I was okay.

I don't believe any person is truly free until they have no need to impress anyone else. It feels so good to be free from the agony of insecurity and have nothing to prove.

False Security

Anything that we trust in which can be taken away from us brings insecurity. Only that which cannot be taken away from us brings security.

Source Unknown

What are you clinging to for your security? How stable is it? Are you willing to let it go and totally trust in God? Just so there is no misunderstanding, I am not saying that we should not trust people, employers, banks, or other things that may help us in life, but the truth is that we have no guarantee that they won't fail. The only lifetime guarantee we can have is found in Jesus.

We can trust other things, but we dare not give them the trust that belongs only to the Lord. I trust my husband and I depend on him, but I also know that as long as I have God, I could go on in life even if something happened to Dave. I trust my friends, but I have been deeply hurt by other friends whom I have trusted in the past, so I don't trust them to the point of putting all of my confidence in them. I realize that they could disappoint me, but as long as I have God, I will recover and go on.

I have money in the bank, and I have done my best to choose a bank with a great reputation because I don't want to lose my money, but even if I did, I know I could still be happy. There was a time when I didn't have the money I have now and I was happy then, and I would survive joyfully without it again if I had to. We must learn to enjoy things without developing too strong of an attachment to them. Truthfully, the world and all that is in it is shaky, and we will only end up hurt and disappointed if we put our trust in it. *Anything that we think we need in order to be happy, other than God, is something the devil can use against us!*

God often shakes the worldly things that we have our trust in. He does it in order to get us redirected toward Him. He is doing us a huge favor when He does this because sometimes we can have too much of our trust in things and not even realize it.

Self-Reliance

Are you trusting in yourself? We all do until we learn that due to the inherent weakness of the flesh, we will always end up disappointed in ourselves. We often feel that we can't trust anyone except ourselves, so we try desperately to take care of ourselves, and when we do we miss out on the amazing protection of God. After many years of being in self-protection mode and experiencing a lot of fear, I finally retired from self-care and turned the task over to God. What a relief to discover that if I cast my care on Him, He will take care of me (see 1 Peter 5:7).

We may seek to feel secure in our own self-righteousness. We try to do the right thing so we can feel good about ourselves, but that is not God's plan. God wants us to feel good about ourselves, not merely because we do the right thing, but because He loves us and has made us right with Him through Jesus Christ.

> . . . The righteousness of God which comes by believing with personal trust and confident reliance on Jesus Christ (the Messiah) . . .
>
> Romans 3:22

The apostle Paul wrote in his letter to the Philippians of how he once trusted in his own righteousness for his worth and value. He said that he had grounds to rely on himself more than any man. He kept the law and was a very religious man. He was from the right neighborhood, had the right education, the right friends and connections. He even said that it was difficult to find anything wrong with him (see Philippians 3:4–6). He was smug in his own self-righteousness until God revealed to him that true righteousness is only found through Christ. After receiving that revelation from God, he declared that everything he thought he had before was all rubbish compared to knowing Christ Jesus as his Lord. He wanted to be found and known as in Christ, not having any self-achieved righteousness based on his own ability (see Philippians 3:8–9). When we make this transition from trusting ourselves to trusting God, we enjoy a freedom and a type of rest that we have never known before.

Are you wearing yourself out trying to take care of yourself? If so, you can also retire from self-care and start truly enjoying life. God wants us to totally depend on Him because He is the only one who can be totally depended on to take care of us and give us what we need. We are all quite independent, but the Holy Spirit works in us until we are totally dependent on God. I suggest that you begin each day by remembering that you need God in all that you do, and that without Him you will not be truly successful. Tell God that you need Him and that you are choosing to put your trust in Him rather than in yourself or anything else. This will help you position yourself properly before you even begin the day.

Paul spoke of times when their troubles were so intense that they felt they had received the very sentence of death, but that it was to keep them from trusting in themselves instead of on God (see 2 Corinthians 1:8–9). At times God must allow our troubles to be more than we can possibly handle on our own so we will ultimately realize our need for Him. If you feel right now that what is going on in your life is more than you can bear, you don't see a way out, and you absolutely don't know what to do, then you are in a good place. You now know that the only thing you can do is trust God, and that is exactly what He wants. God wants us to be totally dependent on Him. Jesus said, "Apart from me you can do nothing" (John 15:5 NIV). It takes us a long time to fully realize that, and in order to, we often have to go through many difficult and disappointing things on our journey from independence to total dependence on God.

We see a good example in Job's life. Job was a godly man, but he had self-righteousness issues. He thought so highly of himself that he even dared to find fault with God. God allowed enough difficulty to come into his life that he finally realized only God is truly righteous at all times. Job came to the end of his own wisdom and righteousness and finally said in reply to God's confrontation, "Behold, I am of small account and vile! What shall I answer You? I lay my hand upon my mouth" (Job 40:4). We must fully realize that God is everything and we are nothing without Him, and only then can we receive Him in the full measure of all He desires to give to us. God certainly didn't want Job to feel bad about himself, but it was necessary for him to come to the realization that he was nothing apart from God, and certainly not wiser than God in any way.

The Exchanged Life

When we enter a relationship with God through Jesus Christ, we are offered an exchanged life. We give Him everything we are and everything we are not, and He gives us everything He is. We give Him our sin and He gives us His righteousness; we give Him our fears and insecurities and He gives us His faith and security. Being a Christian is much more than having our sins forgiven and trying to be good so we can go to Heaven when we die. It is a glorious life of freedom, love, faith, righteousness, hope, joy, and peace. It is a life of accomplishment and bearing good fruit through Jesus that glorifies Him.

When we are insecure we try to do good things so we can feel good about ourselves and be admired by people, but when our security is in Christ, we do what we do through Him and for Him alone. A life in Christ is an entirely new way of living!

Freedom

When our security is found in Christ and we no longer feel that we have to perform in order to have value, we are set free from many fears. As long as we have deep-rooted fears about ourselves and our worth and value, we will have fear in most areas of life. Knowing who we are in Christ and accepting and loving ourselves only because God accepts and loves us is amazingly wonderful. When we know that we are weak in ourselves, then we don't expect something from ourselves that we are not able to do. I know that I will make mistakes, that I need help from other people and from God, and nothing I can do will make me a success in life unless God gives me His undeserved favor. We must know beyond a shadow of a doubt that without Christ we are nothing, and that in us (our flesh) dwells no good thing. We are useless without God! But with Jesus, we can do all things—we are strong in Him, accepted in Him, made right with God through Him, justified in Him, and forgiven through Him. It feels so good not to feel pressured to impress anyone! Our worth is in Christ, not in what other people think of us.

> Our worth is in Christ, not in what other people think of us.

Insecurity produces fear, worry, and anxiety, but security produces boldness and courage. Insecurity produces frustration, struggle, restlessness, and fatigue, but security produces rest, peace, and joy. Insecurity produces an inability to make decisions, but the person who is secure is decisive. Insecurity produces avoidance of others and isolation, but security produces love, confidence, and good relationships.

Insecurity is very hard on relationships. When one person feels that they must constantly try to make the other person feel good about themselves, it steals their freedom. They cannot be honest, and eventually, they get so weary that they may feel that keeping the relationship is not worth the work it takes. When we are in relationship with an insecure person we find that their needs are abnormal. They need an unusual amount of encouragement, and we have to constantly be careful not to hurt their feelings. Although we all like to be made to feel valuable, when we are secure in Christ, we get what we need from Him. His love and acceptance make us feel special and valuable even when people don't.

Most of our unhappiness and frustration in all areas of life can be traced back to our own insecurities, but thankfully we have an answer in Jesus.

Going Forward

Choose an area in your life in which you experience insecurity and pray about it. Make a decision to give your fears to God and receive His grace to enable you to be full of faith in that area. Be sure to remember that we don't usually overcome a problem overnight, but rather little by little. The Lord told the Israelites that He would defeat their enemies little by little so that the beast of the field would not increase among them. My personal belief is that "the beast" is pride. As we humble ourselves under God's mighty hand, we receive His grace and experience His freedom.

> *And the Lord your God will clear out those nations before*
> *you, little by little; you may not consume them quickly, lest*
> *the beasts of the field increase among you.*
>
> Deuteronomy 7:22

Read, study, and meditate on God's Word about being free from fear and secure in Him. His Word will renew your mind, and fear will turn to faith and courage. Take the steps of faith that God leads you to take even though you might still feel some fear, and as you go forward you will begin to sense more and more freedom. For example, if you would love to apply for a position that would be a promotion for you in your company, but have been too insecure and fearful to do so, step out and try it. Even if you don't get the position, you will have been successful in stepping out in faith, and that is the most important thing.

One of the keys to success is to never give up. Even though we may not sense any change after we have prayed, it is vitally important that we continue believing in God's promise to deliver us from a life of fear. When the Holy Spirit is walking me out of bondage into freedom in any area, I often say that I am free from a thing even while I am still experiencing no freedom at all. By doing this, I am declaring my belief that God and His promise are greater than my problem and that it is only a matter of time before I experience the fullness of His freedom. He has never failed me and He will never fail you either. Believe in your heart and, at the right time, you will see with your eyes! Joy is released in our lives through believing. Once we choose to believe God's Word, we receive joy and peace, and that helps us enjoy life while we are waiting for the fullness of God's promise to manifest.

I am sure that the idea of believing what you cannot see or feel may be a bit foreign to you unless you have already learned this powerful biblical principle. If it is, I totally understand. We live in a world where everything is based on seeing and feeling. God's kingdom operates on an entirely different principle, and as citizens of His domain, we are required to believe first and see later. You may be thinking, *Joyce, I just can't do that*, but I know from experience that you can decide to believe what you want to if you stop letting your thoughts and emotions rule you. Doubt may attack you, but you can be like Abraham of whom it was said, "No unbelief or distrust made him waver (doubtingly question) concerning the promise of God..." (Romans 4:20). You can doubt your doubts instead of believing them!

You can doubt your doubts instead of believing them!

Choose to believe right now that you are on your way to enjoying complete freedom from all insecurity. You are making a journey. I cannot tell you exactly how long it will be, but I do know that God is faithful and His promises are for all who will choose to believe them. You do not have to live in the agony of the fear that you are not able or acceptable, because the truth is that you can do all that God wants you to do through Jesus Christ. His strength is yours if you will humble yourself and receive it.

CHAPTER 7

Keep Your Eyes on the Prize

Do you not know that in a race all the runners compete,
but [only] one receives the prize? So run [your race] that
you may lay hold [of the prize] and make it yours.

1 Corinthians 9:24

I am a very goal-oriented person and I have learned that there are several very important things that I need to do in order to reach my goal. If you have goals or dreams for your life, they won't merely happen because you want them to; you will need to do certain things. If we compare reaching our goals to a runner running a race to win, the first thing I believe we need to do is understand that each runner has a running style all his own. To me, that means we must be ourselves and not try to copy someone else. David wanted to kill Goliath and, after a time of being against the idea, King Saul finally told David that he could try, but he wanted David to wear his armor. David tried to go in Saul's armor, but he was uncomfortable and realized that it wasn't going to work for him.

> *Then Saul clothed David with his armor; he put a bronze*
> *helmet on his head and clothed him with a coat of mail.*
> *And David girded his sword over his armor. Then he tried*
> *to go, but could not, for he was not used to it. And David said*

to Saul, I cannot go with these, for I am not used to them. And
David took them off.

1 Samuel 17:38–39

In order to reach our goals, you and I must follow God's leading. People will offer us a lot of advice, and some of it may be good, but some of it may not. Or it may be good advice, but simply not what will work for us. God has created us as unique individuals, and He does not lead all of us in the same way. So, if you want to win your race, you will need to find your own running style or your own way of doing things. Of course we can learn from other people, but we dare not try to copy them at the cost of losing our own individuality.

> God has created us as unique individuals, and He does not lead all of us in the same way.

The next thing we must do to reach our goals is keep our eyes on the prize. After God told Joshua that he was to finish leading the Israelites into the Promised Land after the death of Moses, He said several very important things to Joshua. In the first nine verses of Joshua chapter 1, we find these instructions: Be strong (confident) and of good courage; turn not to the right hand or the left so that you may prosper wherever you go; and keep speaking and meditating on the Word of God.

And then—once again—Joshua is told to be strong, vigorous, and very courageous, be not afraid, neither be dismayed. God was obviously warning him that fear would come to him, but his reaction should be to "fear not." He may have felt fear, but he couldn't give in to it. He had to keep pressing forward no matter how he felt.

If this is the formula for success, then we should pay very close attention. God had already laid out the plans for the Israelites' successful entry into the Promised Land. He said, "Every place upon which the sole of your foot shall tread, that have I given to you, as I promised Moses" (Joshua 1:3). All Joshua needed to do was to begin walking toward the goal in faith and not quit until he had succeeded. Of course he needed to be courageous, bold, confident, and fearless if he was to do that, but he was also told to keep his eyes on the prize and not look to the right or the left. That statement indicates that he had to maintain strong focus on the goal in order to reach it.

We all have circumstances in our lives that can derail us and prevent us from reaching our goals if we pay excessive attention to them. Do what the crisis demands, but don't give it undue attention. Keep your conversation full of your goals, not your problems.

Scripture teaches us to look away from everything that will distract us unto Jesus who is the Author and the Finisher of our faith (see Hebrews 12:2). I believe that it is God who plants goals, dreams, and visions into our heart, and we need to follow His guidance in order to see them brought to completion. Our enemy, the devil, seeks to prevent our progress by providing trials and problems that will distract us if we let them. I realize that we cannot completely ignore our problems. There are things that demand our attention and we need to take care of them. Let's learn to do our responsibility and cast our care upon the Lord. Most problems can be handled rather quickly if we do what we can do and choose not to worry about the rest. We are to do what the crisis demands and cast our care on God (see 1 Peter 5:7; Ephesians 6:13).

I encourage you to have the heart of a finisher. Make a decision from the beginning of your goal that you will finish no matter how difficult it is or how long it takes. Keeping our eyes on the prize makes the difficult times easier. We need to believe that the reward will come if we don't give up. Jesus endured the cross for the joy of the prize that was set before Him (see Hebrews 12:2). To "endure" means to outlast the problem. Whatever problem you might be facing right now will eventually pass, so while the problem is still screaming at you, keep your eyes on your goal and look forward to winning your race and the prize of victory.

Even when I get very tired of going to the gym three times a week to lift weights and push my body in order to build muscle, I think about how much better I look and feel and how much better my clothes fit me when I am diligent in going. Keeping my eyes on the prize helps me reach my goal.

When I get weary from always being responsible for something, traveling and staying in hotels, and having jetlag, I keep my eyes on the prize of eventually standing before God and hearing Him say, *"Well done thou good and faithful servant."* I also remember there are lots of people who still need to know the Lord, and that helps me to be determined to finish my race.

The same principle applies in your life. If you are in debt and your goal is to be debt-free, then you should keep the prize in mind of how wonderful it will be to have no debt when you get tired of disciplining yourself not to make purchases you can do without. When you get tired of going to work every day, think about the prize of your paycheck and being able to pay your bills and have food to eat.

If you're on a diet and tired of not being able to eat everything you want, keep your eyes on the prize of being able to fit into the clothes that you hid in the back of your closet, hoping that someday you would be able to wear them again.

> *Don't throw away your dreams in a moment of discouragement or weariness. Keep your eyes on the prize!*

Don't throw away your dreams in a moment of discouragement or weariness. Keep your eyes on the prize!

Don't Look Around, Down, or Back

God's Word tells us not to look to the right or the left, and that means don't look around you. The prophet Isaiah instructed people not to look around them in terror.

> *Fear not [there is nothing to fear], for I am with you; do not look around you in terror and be dismayed...*
>
> Isaiah 41:10

If we look around at our circumstances excessively, we may end up terrified and dismayed, which means that we feel there is no way out of our problems or no way to reach our goals. With God there is always a way, because He is the Way!

God's Word tells us to look up, for redemption is drawing close (see Luke 21:28). If we are to look up, then that means we should not look down. God told Lot and his wife not to look back at Sodom and Gomorrah (see Genesis 19:17). The apostle Paul states that the one thing most important to him was to look away from what was behind to what was ahead (see Philippians 3:13). Look forward to the good things ahead—this will keep you encouraged.

> *Let your eyes look right on [with fixed purpose], and let your gaze be straight before you.*
>
> Proverbs 4:25

We look at things in our thinking. We can look any direction we choose to, so why wouldn't we choose to look at something that will keep us encouraged? We can imagine and see the good things that we are working toward even before we can see them with our natural eyes.

God also told Abraham to look up. Abraham and Sarah had no children, yet God had told him that He would make of him a great nation. How could that be? While they were waiting, Abraham complained to God about having no children. The Lord told Abraham to go outside his tent and to look at the stars, and if he could count them, that would be how many descendants he would eventually have (see Genesis 15:3–5). Wow! Abraham didn't even have a child, so how could he have descendants? He and Sarah needed a miracle, because without one there was no hope of them having a child. I am sure that Abraham's faith was tested and he felt afraid when he looked at his own body that was impotent, and Sarah's, which was also too old to have children. He was in his tent, probably weary of looking at his circumstances, and God brought him out of his tent and told him to look up instead of around at his circumstances.

I think there is an important lesson in this example. Sometimes we can just get out of the house and go for a short walk and things will seem better. When you are weary and losing sight of your goals, go and have a cup of coffee with a friend—and make it someone who is encouraging. Quite often little things can make a big difference. Don't discourage yourself by staring at your problems. Let's merely glance at our problems, but fix our gaze on Jesus!

Sometimes we need to get away from circumstances and get a fresh vision. Looking at the stars often reminds us of the greatness of God. Do whatever you need to do to keep a fresh vision of your goals. Run your race to win and keep your eyes on the prize.

Have the Heart of a Finisher

It is easy to begin a new thing. When something is new, it is exciting, and at the beginning, we have no idea how long it will take or how difficult it might be to see it all the way through to the finish. I don't get excited anymore just because people tell me about a new thing they are beginning. I encourage them, but I don't assume that they will finish just because they have begun. Sadly, my experience has been that there are lots of people who get a great idea, a goal, or a dream, and they begin, but somewhere along the way they turn back. The way becomes difficult and it is taking too long, so they quit and wait for something easier in life to come along. I believe you can be a finisher, but you will have to be determined! I want to encourage you to set your mind and keep it set on finishing your race and obtaining the prize.

Now, I don't want to sound discouraging or negative by what I am about to say, but most things take longer than we thought they would, are more difficult than we had imagined, and cost us more than we planned. Even if we are dreamers, we must look at things realistically. Jesus told those who were planning to build a building to take time first to count the cost to see if they had what was required to finish.

> For which of you, wishing to build a farm building, does not first sit down and calculate the cost [to see] whether he has sufficient means to finish it?
>
> Otherwise, when he has laid the foundation and is unable to complete [the building], all who see it will begin to mock and jeer at him,

Saying, this man began to build and was not able (worth enough) to finish.

Luke 14:28–30

It is important for everyone to have the heart of a finisher, but I believe it is especially important for God's children. After all, we represent Him, and He always finishes what He starts. Is there anything in your life that you are tempted to give up on? If there is, I am asking you to reconsider. Pray and ask if God wants you to give up, and unless you are sure that He does, I recommend that you press on. The only reason we should ever give up is if we realize somewhere along the way that we are not doing what God wants us to do.

Don't let the fear of circumstances or the weariness of passing time cause you to give up. You might be tired of waiting, but I want to suggest that pressing forward is much better than going back. The Israelites frequently wanted to return to Egypt because the things they encountered frightened them and were not easy, but eventually some of them did make it to the Promised Land. Some of them finished their race and won the prize. They didn't all make it, but those who had the heart of a finisher did.

> *Pressing forward is much better than going back.*

The Dissatisfaction of Quitting

Jesus said that He found satisfaction in doing the will of His Father and finishing His work (see John 4:34). I wonder how many people in the world are dissatisfied simply because they gave up on their dreams. We should not be people who are easily defeated. I really believe that if we stay close to God we can press through things that oppose us. He gives us the grace (power of the Holy Spirit) to do whatever we need to do in life. Don't merely try to push through difficulties in the strength of your own flesh, but learn to be thoroughly dependent on God. He gives grace to those who are humble enough to receive it, but if we want to try it on our own, He will wait for us to exhaust our own efforts.

We can only find true satisfaction in doing the will of God. People often ask me when I am going to retire, and I find it to be an odd question. I never considered retirement because I don't know how one can retire from a call God has placed on their life. I will change how I do things in order to get the rest I need as my age increases, but I don't plan to quit. I am determined to finish my course! I want God to be proud of me, and I want to get my full reward when I cross the finish line.

Read what Jesus said about finishing:

> I have glorified You down here on the earth by completing the work that You gave Me to do.
>
> John 17:4

Jesus asked for His prize, so to speak, when He asked to be glorified. He wanted to return to the former glory He had before coming to the earth to pay for our sins (see John 17:5). He clearly said that He qualified for the prize because He finished the work He was sent to do. He said this because He had the heart of a finisher, even though He had not died on the cross yet and been resurrected from the dead. There was no thought at all of quitting. He still had many difficult things to go through, and I am sure that He felt all the fears that we experience, and yet He knew that He would finish.

The example of Jesus challenges and inspires us to become

finishers too. No matter how difficult our task seems, we can have the heart of a finisher because the same Spirit that raised Christ from the dead dwells within us (see Romans 8:11). Let me encourage you to ask yourself, *Have I set my mind to finish?* If the answer is no, why not do it right now? Today—and every day moving forward—pray that you will be the kind of person who always finishes what they start.

Obstacles

God doesn't remove every obstacle that could possibly prevent us from finishing our race and obtaining our prize; as a matter of fact, there are times when He places obstacles in our path in order to test and strengthen our faith. We are strengthened as we deal with difficulties, but if we run from all of them, we will never grow and become stronger in our faith and abilities.

A Butterfly

A man found a cocoon for a butterfly. One day a small opening appeared. He sat and watched the butterfly for several hours as it struggled to force its body through the little hole. Then it seemed to stop making any progress. It appeared as if it had gotten as far as it could and could go no farther. Then the man decided to help the butterfly.

He took a pair of scissors and snipped the remaining bit of the cocoon. The butterfly then emerged easily. Something was strange. The butterfly had a swollen body and shriveled wings. The man continued to watch the butterfly because he expected at any moment that the wings would enlarge and expand to be able to support the body, which would contract in time. Neither happened. In fact, the butterfly spent the rest of its short life crawling around with a swollen body and deformed wings. It was never able to fly.

What the man in his kindness and haste did not understand was that the restricting cocoon and the struggle required for the butterfly to get through the small opening of the cocoon are God's way of forcing fluid from the body of the butterfly into its wings so that it would be ready for flight once it achieved its freedom from the cocoon. Sometimes struggles are exactly what we need in our lives.

If God allowed us to go through all of life without any obstacles, it would cripple us. We would not be as strong as we could have been. Many times our obstacles are what God uses to give us the strength to fly, as long as we refuse to quit when there seems to be no way to go on. You can face your fears and overcome them, and when you do, you'll often find them turning into a blessing.

God's Word says in Romans 8:37 that we are more than conquerors. To me that means we choose to believe we can overcome anything that stands in our way with God's help. It is amazingly freeing and good to trust that you can overcome problems before you even get them.

Are you dreading things that have not even taken place yet? If you are, you don't have to because you can adopt the attitude of an overcomer. You can replace those dreads with a confident attitude that says, "No matter what comes my way in life, I can face it and overcome it with God's help." Will you decide today to have the attitude of an overcomer? If you have this confidence you can live without allowing fear to rule your decisions in life. This confident attitude eliminates dread in our lives, and that in turn sets us free from fear. Fear always begins with a feeling of dread and shrinking back from difficulty instead of boldly going forward. Dread is "baby fear." It is not fully grown yet, but it will develop into full-grown fear if we feed it with wrong thinking and attitudes. Resist the devil at his onset by refusing even a minor dread and replacing it with an attitude that declares, "I can do all things through Christ who strengthens me" (see Philippians 4:13).

Always remember: Don't look to the right or the left, don't look back, don't look down in discouragement or despair, but look up and ahead at the prize that is waiting for those who go all the way through to the end fulfillment of their dreams.

CHAPTER 8

The Creative Power of Fear and Faith

"...It shall be done for you as you have believed..."

Matthew 8:13

Both fear and faith contain creative power. By faith God created the world that we live in. By faith Sarah conceived and gave birth to a child even though she was far too old to do so. Many people have done seemingly impossible things by faith. They have received strength beyond their natural ability, as when Samson killed 1,000 men with the jawbone of a donkey (see Judges 15:16). History tells of those who believed in God that were burned at the stake while they sang praise to God. I, for one, don't know how that would even be remotely possible without a strong faith in God. I know for sure that fear didn't urge them to sing while they were burning.

Faith is leaning entirely on God in absolute trust and confidence in His power, wisdom, and goodness (see Colossians 1:4). Faith believes for something good to happen. It believes that God can do what would be impossible with man. Faith contains creative power.

Faith believes what it cannot see yet. It believes in its heart, not with its eyes. You can choose to believe in your heart that something wonderful is about to happen. Believe that God's power is in you and that you need not fear anything because He has promised to be with you always. Wake up every morning with an enthusiasm for the day. You might not awake every day feeling especially enthusiastic (I know that I don't) but we can decide to believe and expect good things, and as soon as we do, enthusiasm begins to fill our soul.

You can do something that nobody else on Earth can do exactly the way you can do it. Celebrate your specialness and explore the potential of each day. Don't waste your day shrinking back from life in fear, for today is all we truly have. Be open to all your possibilities and above all, always believe in miracles!

Do You Believe?

One day a six-year-old girl was sitting in a classroom. The teacher was going to explain evolution to the children. The teacher asked a little boy if he could see the grass outside. "Yes, teacher, I see the grass." The boy's name was Tommy so the teacher said, "Tommy, go outside and look up and see if you can see the sky. He returned in a few minutes, "Yes, I saw the sky." The teacher asked, "Did you see God?" "No, teacher, I didn't see God." The teacher said, "Well, class, that is my point. We cannot see God because He isn't there."

A little girl spoke up and wanted to know if she could ask the boy some questions. The teacher agreed and the little girl asked: "Tommy, do you see the tree outside?" He responded, "Yes, I see the tree." She asked, "Do you see the grass?" He said, "Yes, I see the grass." "Do you see the sky? Do you see the teacher?" Tommy said, "Yesssss," and his voice tone indicated that he was tired of answering questions. The little girl finally asked, "Do you see the teacher's brain?" Tommy said, "No, I don't see her brain." The little girl said,

"Then according to what we were taught today that means she must not have one." We walk by faith and not by sight (see 2 Corinthians 5:7).

I would venture to say that the six-year-old girl was wiser and probably had more joy than the teacher. If we are only able to believe what we see with our natural eyes, we lack true vision and have no ability to dream. We have no faith, and where there is no faith, fear will always rule and torment.

> *If we are only able to believe what we see with our natural eyes, we lack true vision and have no ability to dream.*

Just as I believe that faith has creative power, I also believe that fear contains creative power. Fear believes that something bad will happen, and we see over and over that if a person consistently believes something awful will take place, then it usually does. Take the example of people who have phobias concerning germs and disease. They are constantly afraid of getting sick, and then the stress of their negative belief frequently makes them sick. Quite often I have witnessed someone experience a problem and then heard them say, "I was afraid that was going to happen," or, "I knew that was going to happen." They had already planned for the problem before they even got it! Some people are afraid they will lose their jobs and they do; others are afraid they will be lonely all their lives and they end up that way. A student might be afraid they will fail a test at school and they do. I have done the same thing in the past, but thankfully God has taught me to expect good things rather than bad ones.

Fear totally blocks our creativity and we are disabled from doing what we are well able to do. The student who fails the test out of fear may have known the material well, but fear disabled him. The employee who was afraid of losing their job may have let fear disable them from doing a good job, so their employer let them go. People who are afraid of being lonely and rejected are unaware that their fear causes them to behave in a way that makes people uncomfortable around them. They may even be unfriendly, which prevents others from befriending them, and it is due to their fear of being rejected.

I am not suggesting that every time a fear presents itself to us that we are in danger of having something bad happen, but I do believe that if a person consistently believes and speaks that bad things are going to happen, they may well be releasing the creative power to make them happen.

After having many difficult and painful things happen in his life, Job said . . .

> *For the thing which I greatly fear comes upon me, and that of which I am afraid befalls me.*
>
> Job 3:25

According to the Bible, our words contain the power of life and death (see Proverbs 18:21). That is a truth that we definitely should not ignore. If you and I can speak life to others, ourselves, and our future, why would we want to speak death? We do not really want to, but due to being deceived about the power of our words, we open our mouth and speak out all of our thoughts and emotions without realizing what we are doing and the power that those words have.

If individuals are afraid, then they will speak fearful things out of their mouths, and those words can adversely affect their lives. Fearful thoughts and words block our ability to hear from God, and we can fall into harm's way simply because we are not acting wisely. We need to be led by the Spirit of God and walk in His wisdom. In order to do that we need faith, not fear. We receive everything from God only by faith, and likewise we can receive the negative and bad things that Satan has planned for us through fear. I realize that most people prefer not to even think about the devil, let alone believe that he is alive and well on planet Earth and has the capability of adversely affecting our lives. We are sure to be defeated if we don't know our enemy. There are many Scriptures that teach us about the reality and work of Satan (the devil):

> *Be well balanced (temperate, sober of mind), be vigilant and cautious at all times; for that enemy of yours, the devil, roams around like a lion roaring [in fierce hunger], seeking someone to seize upon and devour.*
> *Withstand him; be firm in <u>faith</u> [against his onset...].*
>
> 1 Peter 5:9 [emphasis mine]

> *So be subject to God. Resist the devil [stand firm against him], and he will flee from you.*
>
> James 4:7

These two Scriptures make it clear that we need to resist Satan and that we can only do so through faith. If we allow fear to rule in our lives, we are giving the devil an opportunity to work. We are instructed to be cautious at all times and vigilant in our resistance to the devil, and that includes aggressively resisting fear. We cannot be passive, for if we are, we will be taken advantage of. We can resist fear, and it is not difficult to do once we learn to walk in faith at all times. In each situation, we can choose to believe God's Word instead of the thought or emotion of fear that is being provoked by Satan. Remember, according to God's Word, "God has not given us a spirit of fear, but of power and of love and of a sound mind" (2 Timothy 1:7 NKJV).

Deception

And the huge dragon was cast down and out—that age-old serpent, who is called the Devil and Satan, he who is the seducer (deceiver) of all humanity the world over...

Revelation 12:9

Satan is a deceiver. The book of Revelation tells us of a time when Satan will be cast out and down, but for now he is still deceiving people. In the *Vine's Greek Dictionary*, the word "deception" is defined *to cheat, that which gives a false impression, whether by appearance, statement, or influence.* The feelings and thoughts of fear give a false impression. We receive, as a probable reality, something bad that isn't in existence. Fear is filled with thoughts of "what if," and the mental images we conjure up are never anything pleasant.

The Bible mentions deception in connection with many things. For example, it speaks of the deception of riches. Many people think that their security is in their riches, and then they become afraid of losing them.

Satan also tries to lure us into self-deceit, and it is said to be a sin against common sense. Self-deceit leads a person to think more highly of themselves than they should, and that can hinder them from total dependence on God. Self-deception can lead us to be so self-reliant that we become afraid to trust anyone or anything except ourselves. We are also deceived when we think God accepts us because of our good work. It is our faith in Jesus that makes us acceptable to God, and not because we keep all the rules and laws of religion. If we think we must keep all the rules to be accepted, the by-product of that deception is that we become afraid of God's anger when we don't keep the rules and behave perfectly. I think it is safe to say that all deception leads to fear in some way, which is of course Satan's main goal.

Overcoming Fear with Faith

Faith is the only true antidote for fear. If a person unknowingly swallows poison, as soon as they become aware of it, or begin to experience adverse symptoms, they look for the antidote. An antidote has the power to reverse something harmful. Fear is harmful and as soon as we sense the adverse effects of it, we should immediately return to faith. We can always overcome fear with faith. We recognize fear and keep going forward with God, knowing that our faith in Him is greater and will produce much better results than the fear.

> *We can always overcome fear with faith.*

Fear has symptoms. It makes us tense and nervous. We cannot relax or truly enjoy anything that we are doing. If I were at a party, but was afraid that some of the people there didn't like me, then I wouldn't be able to relax and enjoy myself. That would be a mild reaction compared to some of the experiences I have heard about. People can get such intense physical symptoms from fear that they need to go to the hospital due to feeling that they cannot breathe or feeling that they are having a heart attack. This type of reaction is called an anxiety or a panic attack. Some people have these attacks and unless they are caused by a chemical imbalance in their body, they are always connected in some way to fear. Often the root cause is difficult to locate because the fear may be due to something that happened to them in their childhood that they have blocked out of their consciousness and can no longer remember.

Other symptoms of fear would include shrinking back from a challenge instead of facing it boldly. Feeling incapable instead of capable. Always sticking with things that are familiar rather than stepping out into anything that would be adventurous or new. There is a long list of physical symptoms one might experience as well. Fear has dangerous and devastating symptoms, but we have the antidote, and it is faith in God!

You're Not Alone

You are not alone! God is with us, and because of that we can conquer fear. God assigns angels to each of us to watch over and protect us, and we have the Holy Spirit with and in us at all times.

> For [the Spirit which] you have now received [is] not...to put you once more in bondage to fear...
>
> Romans 8:15

The Holy Spirit is our constant companion! That makes me feel safe, and I pray that it does you also. I think it is a great thing to realize that we are not alone. Because honestly, quite often we do feel alone. We think that nobody understands us, or our problems, and that there is no one to help us. The aloneness that we sometimes feel feeds the feelings of fear.

When Jesus was being tempted by the devil for 40 days and nights in the wilderness, angels came and continually ministered to Him (see Mark 1:13). When He was suffering and facing His most difficult time in the Garden of Gethsemane, He was strengthened by an angel (see Luke 22:43), and He was enabled to press into His heavenly Father's plan. All throughout Scripture we see angels ministering to and being with God's people. Perhaps we need to become more aware that we have ministering and guardian angels with us always.

> For He will give His angels [especial] charge over you to accompany and defend and preserve you in all your ways [of obedience and service].
>
> Psalm 91:11

We have a promise from God that as we obey and serve Him, He will not only be with us Himself, but He will give His angels a special charge over us. We should be more conscious and aware of this promise and perhaps even say out loud a few times a day in our private moments, "I have angels with me right now!"

I heard a story about a girl who was swimming in the ocean when she got into a swell and realized she was in terrible trouble. She was too far out for anyone to get to her, and her friends watched helplessly from the shore as she thrashed about trying to save herself. Suddenly a very tall man appeared in the water with her, but he was standing on top of the water, not swimming in it. He swooped her up, and walking on the water, he carried her to shore and lay her down. Her friends first ran to her to make sure she was breathing, and a few seconds later when they looked for the man, he was gone. They were sure they had seen an angel.

I also heard of a woman who was driving down the road thinking about her daughter who had recently died when she heard her tire pop. She stopped and got out of the car to assess her situation and realized she was a long way from any help. As she looked up she saw a man in the distance coming toward her rolling a tire. He said, "I have been sent to help you." He changed her tire and as he walked away he turned back and said, "Jenny is fine and you don't need to worry about her anymore." Jenny was her daughter who had died. Surely, the visitor who was sent to help her was an angel.

There are literally thousands upon thousands of reports such as these, and it is quite exciting and comforting to realize that we truly are not alone. God sends His angels to assist us in many ways that we probably don't recognize.

> *Are not the angels all ministering spirits (servants) sent out*
> *in the service [of God for the assistance] of those who are to*
> *inherit salvation?*
>
> Hebrews 1:14

Perhaps like me, you're not sure that you have ever seen an angel, but we can and should have the faith to believe they are with us simply because God's Word says that they are.

Don't Let Fear Stop You

I have already established that we will all feel fear at various times in our lives, but we don't have to let it stop us. We don't have to obey it. Realizing that we are never alone, but that we in fact have divine help with us at all times, should embolden us to do whatever we need and want to do, even if we have to "do it afraid."

PART 2

Fear manifests in many ways. We would actually have difficulty in counting all the ways that fear finds to hinder and torment people. In Part 1, I have tried to give understanding about what fear is, where it comes from, what our attitude toward it should be, and how we can resist and overcome it.

In this second part, I want to discuss some of the more prominent fears that people experience. You may deal with a fear that I don't cover in the book, but the tools you need to defeat it are the same as with any fear. The best attitude you can have toward fear is, "I will not fear, and I will do what I need or want to do even if I have to do it afraid!"

CHAPTER 9

The Fear of Lack

*... [God] Himself has said, I will not in any way fail you
nor give you up nor leave you without support. [I will] not,
[I will] not, [I will] not in any degree leave you helpless nor
forsake nor let [you] down (relax My hold on you)! [Assur-
edly not!]*

Hebrews 13:5

The fear of lack, or the fear of not having what you need, is possibly one of the biggest fears that people deal with. We have an
inherent need for preservation and spend much of our time in life
taking care of ourselves and our loved ones. If we think we may
not be taken care of, it is easy to let fear fill our thoughts, words,
and emotions, but we don't have to. As believers in Jesus Christ,
we have the privilege of putting our faith in God to meet all of
our needs. And when we do that, faith will conquer fear. God's
Word teaches us that when we seek the Lord, none of us shall
lack any beneficial thing (see Psalm 34:10). There will be no want
to those who truly revere and worship Him.

*O fear the Lord, you His saints [revere and worship Him]! For
there is no want to those who truly revere and worship Him
with godly fear.*

Psalm 34:9

Have you faced times when you wondered if God would really come through and meet your needs? I have, and now that I am on the other side of those times I can assure you that God is faithful. It is always good to be on the other side of difficulty, but that doesn't seem to help us much when we are going through that difficulty. At least not until we have gone through several things and have experienced God's faithfulness. Then and only then can we develop a strong faith that will overcome the fear of lack in our lives.

We live life forward, but we understand it backward. I can look back now and see how most of the really hard things I went through in life have actually worked out for my good and helped to make me the person I am today. I thought at the time that they would kill me, like most of you do, but here I am still alive and doing well. My problems not only didn't kill me, but they made me stronger!

We may not always get what we want, but God will always provide what we need. He does give us the desires of our heart if those desires are in accordance with His will for us. I sometimes find myself feeling afraid that I won't get what I want, or that things won't turn out the way I want them to, and then I remember that God's ways are better than mine and I trust Him to do what is best for me.

> *We may not always get what we want, but God will always provide what we need.*

A Step of Faith

As I sensed God calling me to teach His Word, I knew that I needed to have lots of time to study and prepare before I would be able to help many people. Preparation is very important, and it is something that we must do if we expect to be any good at what we do. I was a young wife and mother of three children at the time and I worked a full-time job, so that left me with very little time to do anything. I cooked, cleaned, shopped, went to Girl Scout meetings, parent-teacher meetings, helped with homework, went to church, volunteered at church for various committees and events, and on and on the list goes.

Eventually I came to believe that God was leading me to quit my job so I could prepare for what I had come to believe would be a future in ministry. However, there was a problem: Our bills added up to more than Dave's income, so if I quit my job, we wouldn't have enough money to even pay the bills, let alone anything extra for all the unexpected things that come up in life. I was afraid to step out in faith and do what I believed I should do.

I wonder: How many of you are facing a situation like that in your life right now? Perhaps many of you; I hope my story will give you courage to "step out and find out" what the future holds.

I would like to say that I courageously took a step of faith without hesitation, but that was not the case. I waited and waited and finally took a part-time job; then I was fired from my part-time job. You must understand that I was a very hard worker and not the type of employee who got fired. You see, God was leading me to quit my job and totally trust Him, but I gave a sacrifice instead of obedience, which still equals disobedience. I did quit a 40-hour-a-week job, but still worked two and a half days a week so I could take care of myself and feel confident that we would have enough money. I said I was trusting in God, but I wasn't "completely" trusting Him, and that was what He needed from me.

We were $40 a month short of having enough money to pay our bills and God was asking me to trust Him, but I had very little experience in doing that, so the thought of it was extremely frightening to me. I realize now that had I not obeyed God then, I wouldn't be doing what I am doing today. I had to trust God for $40 a month before I could trust him for the millions needed today to reach the world through television and other media outlets with the Gospel of Jesus Christ. I wanted to do something great, but I was unwilling to do something small! People like that never succeed. It is only when we are faithful in little things that God can eventually make us rulers over much (see Matthew 25:21).

> *It is only when we are faithful in little things that God can eventually make us rulers over much.*

When I was fired from my part-time job, I realized that God meant business, and I didn't look for another job. I started my journey of trusting God to meet all of our financial needs, and I knew that meant I would need miracles on a regular basis. God did amazing things for our family over a period of six years while I was teaching two small home Bible studies, and I continued studying every opportunity I got. The things God did would seem small to most people, and perhaps in their mind wouldn't qualify for "miracle status," but to us they were miracles. And as we saw the faithfulness of God, it helped us develop an intimate relationship with Him.

Let me quickly say that I am not suggesting that anyone quit working a job in order to prepare for the next thing you believe God wants you to do, unless you have a clear direction from God to do so. What I did was really radical, but I did see God's provision—and we were never late paying a bill once. If God had not provided, then I would have quickly known it was my idea—not God's—and I would have gotten a job very fast. We must always remember that what God orders, He pays for! God was leading me and the evidence was seen in the fact that He provided what we needed.

The money we needed came in differently each time. Once it was a refund on taxes we weren't expecting. Our monthly fee for utilities was lowered and that helped each month. We got things on sale that we were not expecting at the grocery store, and people would bless us with things that we needed. We were invited out to dinner, which saved on groceries, and quite often someone would just hand us a gift of money and say, "I felt that God put it on my heart to bless you with this." Wow! I had never had anything like that happen to me in my life and it was very exciting. Once I needed new dishcloths and had written on my prayer list a request for a dozen of them. A few weeks went by, and then one day the doorbell rang. I opened the door, and a woman I hardly knew held out a stack of dishcloths and said, "I hope you don't think I am crazy, but I felt strongly that God wanted me to gift you a dozen dishcloths." Things like this had never happened before because I never needed it to, and when I did need it, God came through.

For six years I can say that we lived on monthly miracles. I remember going to garage sales with a few dollars and finding tennis shoes that were new for my children, or other items I needed. I could cook hamburger 100 different ways. New clothes for Dave or me were extremely rare, but somehow we always had what we needed. We didn't have everything we wanted, but we did have what we needed. Through it all I learned not to worry so much and to trust more.

Worry does not empty tomorrow of its sorrow; it empties today of its strength.

Corrie ten Boom

One day while studying, I was struck by the fact that when God was leading the Israelites toward the Promised Land, their clothes and shoes didn't wear out. They didn't get new ones, but God miraculously made the ones they had last 40 years. God has many ways of providing for us, and we should be excited about them all.

The reason I share my story with you is to encourage you as you stand in faith, believing God to meet your needs. Just as God provided for me and for my family, He will provide for you and for your family. The exact methods may be different, but His providing nature is the same—He is the same yesterday, today, and forever. All throughout Scripture God shows Himself to be a provider. Whether it is food, shelter, healing, hope, or salvation, He provides everything we need. So be encouraged today; keep your head up and your eyes looking forward. God's provision is on the way.

Sowing and Reaping

Any farmer knows that he cannot reap where he has not sown, and the same principle is true for us. As we give, it is given unto us (see Luke 6:38), so Dave and I never failed to give our tithe and offerings to the work of God. Even when it was very difficult to do so, we did it and we saw the results. God has given us several promises regarding His care for us that we should take time to look at.

> Give, and [gifts] will be given to you; good measure, pressed down, shaken together, and running over . . .
>
> Luke 6:38

[Remember] this: he who sows sparingly and grudgingly will also reap sparingly and grudgingly, and he who sows generously [that blessings may come to someone] will also reap generously and with blessings.

2 Corinthians 9:6

And God is able to make all grace (every favor and earthly blessing) come to you in abundance, so that you may always and under all circumstances and whatever the need be self-sufficient [possessing enough to require no aid or support and furnished in abundance for every good work and charitable donation].

2 Corinthians 9:8

... Whatever a man sows, that and that only is what he will reap.

Galatians 6:7

Bring all the tithes (the whole tenth of your income) into the storehouse, that there may be food in My house, and prove Me now by it, says the Lord of hosts, if I will not open the windows of heaven for you and pour you out a blessing, that there shall not be room enough to receive it.

Malachi 3:10

We should not give merely to get, but we cannot expect to reap where we have not sown. If you give generously to help others and do so with a good attitude, God will always be faithful to meet all of your needs.

> *If you give generously to help others and do so with a good attitude, God will always be faithful to meet all of your needs.*

God once sent a mighty prophet to a poor widow to have his needs met. It was a time of famine in the land, and when he arrived, she told him that she barely had enough for one last meal for her and her son and then they were going to die. I teasingly say that she was not only poor, but she was also depressed and focused on death. Couldn't God have come up with someone better for the prophet? Before, God arranged for him to be fed by ravens bringing him food in the morning and evening. That sounds more exciting to me than a poor, depressed widow who was focused on dying. But God didn't send Elijah to the widow for himself; he was sent there because the widow needed a miracle.

The first thing that Elijah told her to do was feed him, to which she responded that she could not due to her lack. The prophet persisted in his request, and I am sure that even though she complied, she was quite afraid. He had promised her that if she gave to him first, she would have plenty to eat for the remaining days of the famine. Elijah didn't need the widow to give him something, but she needed to give! As soon as she did, the oil in the bottle and the meal in the barrel began to multiply and continued to do so. This entire story is found in 1 Kings 17, and it is definitely worth taking the time to read and study it.

Don't Be Afraid to Give

If the idea of giving your money away is frightening, then start by doing it afraid and eventually you will be able to do it in faith. Say, "Lord I am afraid, but I am going to do this because You want me to, and I love You." The thought of giving money away may even be foreign to some of you, and if it is, I ask that you study God's Word on the subject. I believe you will see that it is a biblical principle that cannot be ignored.

You may feel that you cannot afford to give, but truthfully, you can't afford not to. No farmer expects a harvest unless he plants seed. If we want a harvest of good things in our lives, then we also need to plant seed. If you don't know the principles of giving, you may not even know where to give or what to give to. The Bible says to bring the tithe and offering into the storehouse that there might be meat in God's house. We should give to churches and ministries that are meeting our needs and the needs of others. Give to the poor! Give to finance the preaching of the Gospel! Give to help people who have no one to help them. Form a habit of being a blessing everywhere you go!

God doesn't need our money, so why does He ask us to give it? I believe giving releases something in us that is beautiful. God is a giver, and I think that when we give unselfishly, we are more like God than at any other time in our lives. Giving is one way to resist selfishness and greed. "It is more blessed (makes one happier and more to be envied) to give than to receive" (Acts 20:35). When someone gives us a gift, we only get the gift, but when we give, we get the joy of giving. The tithe represents the first 10 percent of all of our increase. Why tithe? Because if we are willing to give the first portion right off the top in obedience to God, it shows we are putting Him first and trusting Him to take care of the rest. God can make 90 percent go farther than 100 percent would have, but you'll never know if you don't step out and find out.

God's Provision or Coincidence?

To a child of God, His provision appears to be miraculous, but to those who don't have their faith in God, it seems like mere coincidence. I want to live amazed at what God is doing all the time, so I choose to be like a little child in this matter and I hope you will also. Perhaps if you begin to see what God is already doing for you, then it will be easier to trust that He will always meet your needs and that you don't have to be afraid of lack. Someone told me yesterday that I was lucky that I had been able to overcome the abuse in my childhood. I don't believe it was luck; I believe it was and is the goodness of God. The word "luck" suggests that a thing merely happened by chance and there was nothing divine involved, and I don't believe that. Life would be quite dreary if all we had to look forward to was whatever luck we had or didn't have.

We can trust God to take care of us at all times and in every way. God has done so many amazing things in my life that I don't have enough room in this book to share them all, but here are a couple that I remember fondly.

Our ministry was only a few years old and not very large yet, but we still had ministry bills to pay and lived from week to week, trusting God to provide what we needed. Most of the income came in from small conferences and meetings that I conducted locally. I went to the doctor for a regular checkup, and about three weeks later was in the hospital having surgery due to breast cancer. This was sudden and unexpected and we had no time to plan financially for the interval I would be off work. I was home from the hospital, trying not to worry while I was recovering, and one evening the doorbell rang. A local pastor that we didn't know personally was standing outside and proceeded to tell Dave that he was going out of the ministry and had sold his church building and, as the law requires, was distributing the funds to other ministries. He handed us a check for $10,000! That was probably the largest offering we had ever received at that time and was more than enough to get us through until I could go back to work. Luck? To us this was a huge miracle and certainly not something we attributed to coincidence or luck.

Another time Dave and I desperately needed a new car because ours was literally falling apart. We had no possible way to buy one because it was during the days when I had quit my job and we were trusting God for every little tiny thing we needed. One of Dave's brothers, who didn't know how desperate our situation was, called and said that they were getting a new car. Instead of trading in their station wagon that was in good condition, they felt that they wanted to give it to us!

I only tell you these stories to provoke you to believe God for miraculous provision in your own life. Give as God directs you and trust Him to meet all of your needs according to His riches in Christ Jesus (see Philippians 4:19).

The Lord Is My Shepherd, I Shall Not Lack!

Money is certainly not the only thing we can lack. We need strength, ability, wisdom, creativity, relationships, and hundreds of other things. God's Word teaches us that He will provide everything we need as we trust Him to do so. I daily trust God for grace, wisdom, creativity, and strength to do all that I need to do. I don't merely assume that I will have it, or fear that I won't have it; I ask for it. The apostle James said, "You do not have, because you do not ask" (James 4:2). The apostle John said, "Ask, and you will receive, that your joy may be full" (John 16:24 NKJV).

I was a practicing Christian for many years before I learned that God was my Provider in all things. I knew that my sins were forgiven and that I would go to Heaven when I died, but that was about all I depended on God for. In all other areas, I worked hard to try to take care of myself. Of course I was frustrated, confused, and disappointed most of the time because God wants to take care of us. He will actually hinder us from being successful at whatever we're doing until we trust Him to do it for us.

We should trust God for all things! If you need to confront a situation and you're afraid you won't know what to say, then you can ask God to give you the right words at the right time and trust that He will. If you are applying for a job but you're afraid you won't get it, you can ask God for favor and trust that you will get it. I pray for favor all the time. God's favor causes situations to turn out favorably for you when there is no reason for them to, except that God is working on your behalf. If you are lonely, ask God to provide friends for you. The situations in which we need God's help are endless, and life can get very exciting when we let Him into all of those situations and begin expecting to see Him at work in them.

David said that the Lord is our Shepherd and we shall not lack (see Psalm 23:1). A good shepherd takes care of his sheep, and Jesus is called "the Good Shepherd" (see John 10:11–14). God told the Israelites that He would lead them into a land where they would eat food without shortage and lack nothing in it (see Deuteronomy 8:7–10). God's Word to us today is no different from what it was to them. We don't have to fear lack! God will provide whatever you need in any situation. I admit that His timing is not always as speedy as we would like it to be, but He does not fail us. Even when we have to wait for something longer than we want to, we can trust that God's timing in our life is perfect. Although He doesn't always give us everything we want exactly when we want it, He will give us what we need at the right time, and we can rest in that.

The young lions lack food and suffer hunger, but they who seek (inquire of and require) the Lord [by right of their need and on the authority of His Word], none of them shall lack any beneficial thing.

Psalm 34:10

I love this Scripture because it teaches me that my need gives me a right to ask! Wow! We don't have to be perfect or special, we just have to have a need—and when we do, we can approach God in faith based on the authority of His Word, and we will not lack. Just think, instead of being afraid that we will not have enough of what we need, we can have faith that we will have enough. Don't wait until you are experiencing some kind of disaster to start trusting God. I am trusting God right now that He will take care of me, my family, and our ministry and its partners as long as we are here on Earth. Sometimes we wait until we are in deep trouble before we turn to God, and by then, the devil has his roots deeply planted in all areas of our lives, and although God will certainly help us, it may take longer. If that is the case with you, then don't give up. Be patient and go all the way through with God and learn to live by faith instead of by fear.

Scarcity or Abundance

From its opening in Genesis, the Bible tells a story of abundance. In the first chapter, we see God as lavishly creative. He didn't create a few stars, He created so many that they cannot be counted. His oceans are so huge that we cannot see to the end of them from the shore. He created large amounts of animals and plants and flowers and trees. And after He made it all—including man and woman—He said that His creation was very good! Through-out the Bible we see a God of abundance, who called Himself *El Shaddai*, meaning the God of more than enough.

The people held regular feasts to honor and thank God for His abundance. I am not suggesting that scarcity has not come into this fallen and sinful world, but as citizens of God's kingdom and economy, we can still benefit from God's original plan for man. God sets good and evil, life and death, before us and asks us to choose life (see Deuteronomy 30:19). Choose faith instead of fear; trust God for abundance instead of fearing scarcity; believe that God has more than enough of everything to go around and start trusting Him for your portion.

You might say, "I thought we were supposed to be content with what we have." You are right, we are to be content and that means satisfied to the point where we are not disturbed no matter what our circumstances are. But that does not mean that we should not trust God to improve our situation and provide for us abundantly.

I remember when I had a great fear of not having enough. I had learned early in life that I had to take care of myself. My father was a very stingy man and never seemed to want me to have the things that other children and teenagers had. He did provide for my basic needs but refused to buy me things like a class ring, school pictures, a yearbook, or a graduation dress. If I wanted those things I had to find a way to get them myself. I babysat and worked at a local merchandise store in order to have the things I needed. I think the way he treated me left me with a deep-seated belief that I was only worth the least of everything and should only expect what I had to have in order to get by in life. It was easy for me to make the transition into being an adult who was fearful of never having enough. I lived with as little as I could, but when I did need to purchase something, I searched for the best bargain I could find. Looking for good prices is not wrong, but I was excessive to say the least. The fear of not having enough tormented me continually.

Through my relationship with God, I gradually learned to trust Him for abundance. I learned that God wants His children to have the best, not the least. He does exceedingly, abundantly, above and beyond all we dare to hope, ask, or think (see Ephesians 3:20). I encourage you to develop a mind-set of abundance, not scarcity. Trust God to provide for all of your needs and to give you the desires of your heart (see Psalm 37:4). Don't live in the fear of lack, for God promises that He will liberally supply your every need.

> *And my God will liberally supply (fill to the full) your every need according to His riches in glory in Christ Jesus.*
>
> Philippians 4:19

CHAPTER 10

The Fear of Losing Control

Letting go doesn't mean that you don't care about someone anymore. It is just realizing that the only person you have control of is yourself.

Deborah Reber

The fear of losing control is one of the most prevalent fears that people have. This is the fear that if you don't manage to control the outcome of future events, something unpleasant or even terrible may happen. People who suffer from this fear have a lot of stress because trying to control the world and everyone in it is hard work. The stress of being a controller can eventually cause huge problems. It creates a lot of pressure that can develop into health problems, steals our peace and joy, and doesn't foster good relationships.

I know about the agony of being a "controller" because I was one. For many years in my life I only felt safe when I thought I was controlling all my circumstances and the people I was close to. Part of my controlling nature was rooted in selfishness, but a larger part was rooted in fear. I was simply afraid that I would not be taken care of if I didn't control my surroundings, so I made sure that I was in control.

I know now that the problem began in my childhood. My father was a very controlling man who was abusive in many ways. My mother was too afraid to confront him, so she allowed him to not only control her, but my brother and me as well. His control mechanisms were anger, threats, and rejection. We were frequently threatened with the loss of privileges or provision, but mostly we were the recipients of his violent rages and anger that involved yelling, cursing, pushing, shoving, slapping, and even hitting. His anger also ended in his total rejection of the one who had not pleased him. Eventually he would recover from his current bout of displeasure, only to find something else and someone else to be unhappy with.

Because I despised these episodes, I did everything in my power to keep him happy, and that always involved letting him be in control of even the tiniest details of my life.

One would think that since I hated being controlled I certainly would not have become a controller myself, but I did. We do learn behavior patterns from our parents. They become to us the mirror image of what we assume we are to be. I watched my father get his way through anger and control, so as an adult I thought that was the way to get what I wanted.

Obviously, that kind of behavior is not God's way, but at that point in my life I didn't know any other way existed other than what I was doing. God wants us to trust Him to lead and guide us and to keep us safe, rather than us attempting to control circumstances and people. When I finally gave up the job of what I call "self-care," I found a new joy I had not experienced before.

I would like to say that it was easy and happened overnight, but that wasn't the case. Even after I realized my behavior was wrong, I was in the dark about why I behaved the way I did. I couldn't control my behavior

> God wants us to trust Him to lead and guide us and to keep us safe, rather than us attempting to control circumstances and people.

because, even in that, I was still trying to be in control without asking for God's help.

So, here was my problem: I was a controller who was trying to control myself *not* to be a controller! It didn't work. I needed God's help. I needed to trust God with all of my circumstances, all the people in my life, and I especially needed to trust God to change me. That was a lot of trust that I needed and didn't have. I didn't even know how to have it because I had never been able to trust anyone in my life prior to that. My thinking, emotions, and actions were all riddled with the fear of being hurt or taken advantage of.

God's Plan

Man's ways and God's ways are very different from one another. God's ways are better by far, but it takes us a long time to realize that. And then after that, we have to be willing to give up our old ways of doing things.

> *The plans of the mind and orderly thinking belong to man, but from the Lord comes the [wise] answer of the tongue. All the ways of a man are pure in his own eyes, but the Lord weighs the spirits (the thoughts and intents of the heart). Roll your works upon the Lord [commit and trust them wholly to Him . . .].*
>
> Proverbs 16:1–3

Our minds stay very busy planning, and those plans are for what we think will benefit us. God wants us to roll our works (planning and doing) on Him and get His plan instead of pushing ahead with ours. We are encouraged in Proverbs 3:6 to acknowledge Him in all of our ways. When we do, then things work out much better and we have less stress and lots of joy, but it usually takes a while for us to learn God's ways and be willing to submit to them.

My mother-in-law gave me my first Bible when Dave and I got married, and she wrote a Scripture in the front of it:

> Commit your way to the Lord [roll and repose each care of your load on Him]; trust (lean on, rely on, and be confident) also in Him and He will bring it to pass.
>
> Psalm 37:5

I thought it was a nice Scripture, but I had no idea at the time just how far away from doing it I was. I had no idea how much work God would need to do in my heart in order for that Scripture to be a reality in my life. Yes, God's plan is quite different from ours. We often want to decide what to do and then pray that God will make it work, but He wants just the opposite. He wants us to pray first and take no action without His direction and approval. Is God a controller? It could sound like He is, but He is just the opposite. He gives us the ability to make our own decisions, but He does teach us which ones to make in order for life to turn out good.

God will try to guide us, but He won't force us to do the right thing. I have finally learned to deal with my adult children the same way God deals with us. I may offer some advice, although I try to refrain from doing so too often, but when I do, I still realize that they will make their own decisions. And if they decide against what I suggested, then I say nothing more. It is not my job to control them!

Anything God tells us to do or not to do is for our benefit, and if we trust that, then we can follow His advice easier. God's plan is for us to willingly give our will to Him, asking Him to guide and lead us in all matters of life. He wants us to trust Him, and as we do we can enter into His peace and joy. We can then enjoy our lives while He is working on the circumstances and people in our lives, as well as on us and in us. God's guidance leads us away from all that will cause stress and leads us into His rest.

Certainty in a World of Uncertainty

What we want is certainty, but we live in a world of uncertainty. It is this unrealistic demand that creates stress and anxiety. Certainty makes us feel safe, and we all want that. We are safe with God, but we must learn to believe it and trust Him. Trusting God doesn't mean that everything turns out the way we want it to, but it does mean that it turns out the way that it should. God doesn't always lead us the easy way in life. Sometimes He leads us the long, hard route because in the end it will be the one that was best for us. Even when life hurts, God wants us to trust Him.

All things may not be good in and of themselves, but God can work them out for good if we will trust Him to do so.

> We are assured and know that [God being a partner in their labor] all things work together and are [fitting into a plan] for good to and for those who love God and are called according to [His] design and purpose.
>
> Romans 8:28

Waiting for God to do what only God can do is always the most difficult part of trust.

Even if a person believes this promise, it can still take time for the results to manifest in their life. Waiting for God to do what only God can do is always the most difficult part of trust. Our timing and His are usually two completely different things. He promises to never be late and even states that He is not slow as man defines slowness (see 2 Peter 3:9). But usually He isn't early and we do have to wait. During this waiting is when we tend to take over again and try to control something that only God can control. We lose our joy and peace once again and go around the same mountains in life until we finally realize that we must let God be God in our lives! I have finally decided that if God doesn't change a thing (even if that thing is me), then it simply won't get changed. God is well able to do what needs to be done in all of our lives, and we should be still and let Him do it.

Our lives are like a canvas and God is the artist attempting to paint a perfect picture. Just imagine if while an artist was painting, the canvas refused to be still and kept moving about trying to instruct the painter. The project would be a mess; and that is often what happens in our lives.

> Be still and know that I am God...
>
> Psalm 46:10 (NKJV)

Life on Earth won't give up its uncertainty, so it is us who must concede. Life won't change, so we must change. I have heard it said that "If we don't learn to bend, life will break us all." We don't know what will happen tomorrow or, for that matter, in the next ten minutes, but God does. Since He knows, we can be content to know Him and trust Him.

We can learn to exercise the power we do have and control what we can control instead of trying to control what we can never control. We do have the power not to allow fear to rule our actions, and with God's help we can control our reaction to situations even when we cannot control the situation itself. We cannot control the direction of the wind, but we can set our sails to cooperate with it.

You must learn to let go because in reality, you were never in control anyway!

Expect the Unexpected

Learning to expect the unexpected isn't having a negative attitude; it is simply accepting that we cannot control all of life and then trusting that God will enable us to deal with things as they come. When Noah went into the ark, he had to have complete confidence in God because he had no ability to control the direction of the ark since it had no rudder and no sails. He was out of control, and yet God brought him to a place of safety.

I decided to keep a log of the unexpected things that happened to me over an eight-week period of time. I logged 33 things. Thirty-three things that interrupted my plan and that I had to deal with. I had no choice—they were staring me in the face and I couldn't avoid them; I couldn't control them! But I was able to control my response to them, and for me that was a huge accomplishment. There would have been a time in my life when each of those things, most of which were very minor, would have sent me into either depression or ungodly aggression. In other words, I would have gotten angry. I would have been unable to simply trust God to help me deal with each one. Thank God He changes us! I am very excited to know that we don't have to remain the same, but God is daily working with and in us toward positive change.

Not only can we learn to expect the unexpected, but we can refuse to fear the unexpected. We can live with a confident attitude that God will give us the ability to deal with whatever we need to deal with in life. He has promised to never let more come on us than we can bear and to also always provide a way out (see 1 Corinthians 10:13). So I want you to think about this in a different way: Unexpected things add a touch of mystery to our lives, and I think we all want and need that.

Circumstances in life are not the only things that bring things we don't expect, but people also do unexpected things. They fail us when we need them most. They do things we would have never in a million years thought they would do. We are shocked and hurt, but there it is and we have to deal with it. Perhaps we must let go of our idea of what we expected people to be and try to love them the way they are. Is it really people that disappoint us, or is it sometimes our expectation of them that disappoints us? Expecting people to never hurt us is certainly an unrealistic expectation and one that sets us up for disappointment.

Most of our pain in life is what I call "people pain." We all need people, but developing good relationships is certainly not easy. Sometimes we want to let go when we should hold on, and sometimes we want to hold on when we should let go.

Letting Go of Bad Friends

We need safe people in our lives, not ones who are volatile and are merely bombs waiting to explode. We need people who add to our lives, not ones who drain us. If we love or need a person, we often try to control them and make them what they ought to be. If they are hurting us, we try to change them so they are comfortable for us to be with. That doesn't usually work, and when it doesn't we may have to let go.

Some people think that holding on is heroic, but sometimes

letting go is the most heroic thing we can do. This is an area in which we must learn to be led by the Holy Spirit. I don't advocate giving up on people easily, because sticking with someone through difficulty can be just the thing they need in order to change; however, if the relationship is making you sick emotionally and draining you of the energy you need for your life, then letting go may be the only thing you can do. Sometimes letting go is just a decision to stop trying to change them, and at other times it requires walking away. Walking away is not easy, but there are times in life when we must do it.

We cannot always simply walk away from family members, but we can let go of friends who are poisoning our lives if we feel that is what we are supposed to do. I would even say that if you are struggling with close family members who are hard to deal with, then you need safe friends even more. Healthy friendships can build you up and give you courage to deal with the things you must at home. A friend of mine has a special needs child, and she has shared with me how difficult and draining it can be. She loves the child and knows she will be taking care of him forever, and she is committed to doing so, but she needs friends who can add to her life rather than drain her further. She needs friends who are safe.

For many years I took care of my dad, who abused me. He died a few years ago and I am happy to say that he accepted Jesus before he died. I also take care of my mom who is 89 and my aunt who is 86. Although my parents had abused and abandoned me, I could not just walk away. God wanted me to treat them well even though they had failed to be good parents. It is often very draining trying to deal with them because they have lots of health and emotional issues. Because of this and other responsibilities in my life, it is important that I have safe friends who add to my life and not ones who drain me even further. I have learned that laughter restores me, so I enjoy people who are not tense and difficult to please.

I am sure you have heard the phrase, "You can let go of someone, and if they were ever truly yours, they will come back." Sometimes people need some time and space to grow and mature before they are safe friends for us. If you find that you cannot be friends with someone, continue praying for them and never hold any bitterness in your heart toward them. Perhaps someday the relationship can be restored, but always remember that you must have boundaries in your life or you will be taken advantage of.

Live and Let Live

You can be free from the fear of not being in control if you will learn to trust God to be in control. He has an amazing life for you, so be sure that you live it fully. He has a good plan for you and the right people for you

> *You can be free from the fear of not being in control if you will learn to trust God to be in control.*

to be in relationships with, and I urge you to open your heart to Him fully in these matters. Don't miss your life by letting other people control you, and don't try to control them. All you can do is live your life and let them live theirs.

Release all the people in your life to God because, in reality, they belong to Him anyway. When you release them to His loving care, it releases you to enjoy your life. Give them to Him and trust His long-range plan. You may even have to watch people that you love go through some pain that you would love to help them avoid, but sometimes we have to let people make their own mistakes and learn from them.

Let them live their life even if they don't live it the way you would like for them to. Keep praying and remember that God can do more in one second than you can do in a lifetime.

This would be a good time to pray and—one by one—let go of anyone you are trying to control. Even if your intentions are good, you still need to let them go and trust God to do what needs to be done in their life.

CHAPTER 11

The Fear of Not Being Wanted

Human beings, like plants, grow in the soil of acceptance, not in the atmosphere of rejection.

Sir John Powell

Being abused sexually, verbally, mentally, and emotionally as a child and teenager definitely left me afraid that no one would want me as an adult. Fear permeated the very atmosphere that I grew up in. I was afraid that someone, especially my mother, would find out what my dad was doing to me. I was simultaneously afraid that no one would ever find out and I would never be rescued. I was afraid that if they did find out they would blame me, and there was always the nagging fear that maybe the abuse was my fault. Perhaps there was something wrong with me!

I was afraid of my father's intimidation and anger. I was afraid that I might make him angry, and yet when he was angry I couldn't figure out what I did wrong. I was afraid to ask him for anything, not even a dime to get a Popsicle. Wanting things wasn't very popular in our home, so usually I just didn't ask because of fear of making my dad angry. I felt I had to take care of myself and not need very much; but I was only a little girl, and I was afraid I couldn't or didn't know how to do that. I felt a crushing sense of responsibility. I thought I needed to fix everything, but I was very afraid because I didn't know how to do it.

My fears changed as I became an adult, but they were still present. I had the fear of failure, the fear of letting friends into my life—especially close friends—and the fear of being taken advantage of. There were many fears, both big and small, but the one we will deal with in this chapter was a big one for me.

I longed for the day I could leave home and be on my own, away from the abuse I was suffering, and yet I also lived with the fear that I would be alone and unwanted because I felt like damaged merchandise! The fear of not being wanted is experienced by thousands of people, and it fills us with a sadness that can only be known by one who has felt it. We are created for healthy connections, and there is always a part of us that craves it. We want to be loved! We want to be wanted!

> *We are created for healthy connections, and there is always a part of us that craves it.*

My thoughts were, *What man could love and want to marry someone who has been used by their father the way I have been?* This became a fear in my life that eventually caused me to make a mistake and marry the first young man who seemed to have an interest in me. I did not feel peaceful about the union, but the fear of never having anyone and being alone and unwanted caused me to override wisdom and marry him anyway. Our five-year marriage was filled with more pain, rejection, abandonment, and betrayal. Exactly what I did not need after growing up the way I did. The marriage ended in divorce due to infidelity on his part. I existed under layers of pain that caused a great many problems in my life until I finally received the love and acceptance of Jesus and healing for my wounded soul.

In the last year of the marriage, I got pregnant, and while I was carrying his baby he left me and lived with another woman who happened to reside just two blocks from where he and I lived.

Each day, when I drove to work, I drove by the apartment where they were living together and I vividly recall the painful feelings of being unwanted and rejected. Like most people do, I thought something was wrong with me and that I wasn't good enough, otherwise he would not have left me for someone else. She probably wore a size 4 or 6, and she had long blond hair and blue eyes. I had never in my life worn a size 4 and I had ordinary brown hair and brown eyes. As I compared myself with her, I definitely felt lacking in most areas.

The more flaws we see in ourselves, the more we accept rejection as something we deserve. We begin to internalize it and believe there is something wrong with us that caused the rejection. Like most people in a similar situation, my emotional pain was so intense that I could not think rationally or realize that my husband had many problems and wrong behavior patterns that were not connected to me or anything I was, or anything I was not doing. He was that way when I married him, but I was so desperate and fearful of being unwanted that I refused to be honest with myself about him. I believe that literally thousands upon thousands of women and men make this same mistake. The fear of being alone and unwanted is intense and can motivate us to make unwise relationship decisions.

I am sure you can imagine the emotional pain I felt while driving past the apartment—where he was living with another woman—pregnant with his child, going to work to pay the bills that he created and walked away from.

My pregnancy was a terribly lonely time. I couldn't receive any comfort from my parents, and I had no real friends. I was totally dependent upon being able to take care of myself and very fearful about how I was going to do that as I reached the end of my pregnancy. When I could no longer work, I had no money and no place to turn to for help, so the woman who fixed my hair at the beauty shop where I went invited me to live with her and her mom until after I had the baby.

My soul was scarred from fear, abuse, and rejection, and at that time I did not know that God loved me, would never reject me, and actually wanted to restore my soul and make me whole again (see Psalm 23). If you can relate to how I felt during that time, I urge you to believe that God also wants to restore your life and make it something amazingly wonderful. He is knocking on the door of your heart, and all you need to do is say, "Jesus, come in." God's healing in our lives is not an instantaneous thing; it is a process, but it is definitely available to all who will receive it by faith.

> *God's healing in our lives is not an instantaneous thing; it is a process, but it is definitely available to all who will receive it by faith.*

Even if you are afraid to let anyone else into your life right now, you can begin by letting Jesus in, and He will enable you to eventually let others in also. You can enjoy healthy and safe relationships!

After I gave birth to my son alone in a clinic, my husband did show up and took me to live with him at his aunt's house. That only lasted a few short weeks and he was gone again on another escapade with a different woman. I finally found the courage to divorce him, but my circumstances only worsened because I finally had no choice except to go back to my father's house and try to avoid his sexual advances. I lived there for a few months with my son. I worked during the day while my son stayed with a neighborhood babysitter, and I was miserable all the time. Day and night I was haunted with fear and the pain of being lonely, rejected, and unwanted. I felt stuck in a place that I hated and saw no means of escape.

I had received Jesus as my Savior at the age of nine while visiting relatives, but I had no understanding of what was available to me through my relationship with Christ, so I kept all of my problems even though I had Jesus. I was like a millionaire, spiritually speaking, who never went to the bank to cash a check because I didn't know what I had. However, I did pray what I am sure sounded like pathetic prayers, but God heard me. I asked that one day God would send someone to truly love me and take me to church, and eventually Dave Meyer pulled up in front of my parents' house where I was washing my mother's car and the rest is history. It is a story for another time, but he definitely was the answer to the prayers I had prayed in the midst of my pain.

No matter how bad you are hurting, I urge you to pray! Pour your heart out to God and don't worry about sounding eloquent. Tell Him how you feel and be patient as He works in your life. I admit that it is difficult to be patient when you're hurting, but God will comfort you as you remain steadfast in your faith.

Craving Acceptance

I recently met a woman who expressed her gratitude for our television program. She said the Word of God that she received from it brought healing to her family. She went on to tell me that her son had developed a serious eating disorder that had required hospitalization. I asked if he had been insecure, and she said that he was in a band and began to admire the lead singer and compare himself to him. For no apparent reason he became afraid that the time might come when they would not want him in the band, and although he was not overweight at all and very handsome, he decided he should be as thin as the lead singer. He started down the path of eating and then forcing himself to vomit, so he did not retain the calories in the food. This eating disorder has some serious side effects if it is practiced over a long period of time, and it did have devastating effects on him. The stress from his problems ended up causing his mother to have a post-traumatic nerve disorder, and she needed counseling and medical help. All of these problems began with a young man's fear of being unwanted and rejected. It wasn't even a reality, just a fear! Although he didn't know how to at the time, all he would have had to do was resist the fear in the very beginning and he could have avoided all the pain he had personally, as well as the pain caused to his family. Fear is indeed a formidable enemy and one that we must learn to confront.

We were designed and created by God for acceptance and not for rejection. Because it is an inherent need in us, we crave it, and we need to live in an atmosphere of acceptance in order to grow and make progress. What if we are rejected and unwanted by the people in our lives? Although it is painful, we can still choose to receive God's acceptance and know that we are alive because He wants us. *God wants you!* God is the giver of life, and He has created each of us carefully and purposely. No matter who rejects us, God accepts us. And that is enough to enable us to be successful in life. Jesus was rejected and despised, but He focused on God's love for Him.

> No matter who rejects us, God accepts us. And that is enough to enable us to be successful in life.

We should focus on God's acceptance rather than people's rejection. What we focus on becomes the largest thing in our life.

He was despised and rejected and forsaken by men, a Man of sorrows and pains, and acquainted with grief and sick-

ness; and like One from Whom men hide their faces He was despised, and we did not appreciate His worth or have any esteem for Him.

Isaiah 53:3

Jesus came to help people, yet they hated Him without a cause. Was it painful to Him? I imagine it was because He had emotions just as we do. But He did not let the rejection derail Him from the purpose for which He was sent. Satan launches attacks of rejection against us in the hope that the pain of it will weaken us to the point that we will give up, isolate ourselves, and be so afraid of being unwanted that we end up emotionally crippled and unable to maintain healthy relationships or be successful in life. However, knowledge is power, and when we understand what Satan is trying to do and why, then we can more aggressively resist him and have victory instead of being the victim.

We can trust God to give us the acceptance that we crave instead of compromising our values and making unwise choices in order to get it. I have experienced what seems like more than my fair share of rejection in my life: in my childhood from people I trusted and loved, and later as a woman being used by God in ministry. Some of my most intense pain has come from those rejections, but I have recovered by applying the very same principles that I am sharing with you.

God has already provided the total acceptance we crave, and all we need to do is receive it by faith. Are you afraid to believe it might be true? I know that I was for a long, long time. I thought, *What if I believe that God loves me and I am only deceiving myself? What if I believe I am totally accepted by God and it is really just my imagination?* It almost seemed too good to really be true. But we find our proof in God's Word. Even after we decide to believe we are accepted and wanted by God, our feelings don't always agree. We must learn to believe what God says more than we believe how we feel.

We are made acceptable to God through Christ (see Ephesians 2:6). God doesn't love us because we deserve it, but because He is kind and gracious and wants to love us (see Ephesians 2:4–5). The craving we feel for acceptance can be truly met only in Jesus. He doesn't give it only when we are good and withdraw it when we are not. God accepts us because we believe in His Son Jesus Christ, and not because of what we do or don't do (see John 3:18). You are loved, accepted, and wanted!

You Have Been Chosen

We have been chosen by God, picked out as His own in Christ before the foundation of the world (see Ephesians 1:4). Before we had an opportunity to do anything right or wrong, God decided that He wanted us! I want to encourage you to really think about that and not just merely read over it. You have been chosen by God!

I wrote the following in my *Everyday Life* study Bible on page 1,929:

> One of the strongest desires human beings have is to be loved, to be accepted, and to feel that they belong. We want a sense of connection and belonging to something or someone. We want to feel valuable. We cannot be guaranteed of always getting that in our dealings with people, but we can get it from God. Even though God knows everything about us—and I do mean everything—He still chooses us on purpose. According

to Ephesians 1:4, He actually picked us out on purpose to be His very own and to belong to Him. I encourage you to say aloud right now, "I belong to God."

God set us apart for Himself and made provision in Jesus for us to be holy, blameless, and consecrated. We can live before Him in love without reproach. That means we do not have to feel guilty and bad about all of our weaknesses and faults. You and I are no surprise to God. He knew exactly what He was getting when He chose us. God did not choose us and then become disappointed because of our inabilities. God has hope for us, and He believes in us and is working to help us be all that He has in His plan for us.

I encourage you to relax in God's love. Learn to receive God's love. Think about it, thank Him for it, and watch for the manifestation of it in your daily life. God shows His love for us in many ways, but we are often unaware of it. He loves us first so we can love Him and other people. God never expects us to give away something that He has not first given us. His love is poured out into our hearts by the Holy Spirit and He wants us to live before Him in love.

Let love in and let it out. You are destined to be a channel for God to flow through, not a reservoir that merely sits and collects blessings from God. He blesses us and makes us a blessing. Blessings come in and blessings go out. You are special and God has a special and unique plan for you. Get excited about that and rejoice!

Jesus Cheers Even When We Strike Out

Babe Ruth was once baseball's all-time home run king. But did you know that he was also the all-time strikeout champion? He struck out almost twice as often as he hit home runs. He knew that he had to risk striking out in order to hit those home runs. When asked for the secret of his success, Ruth replied, "I just keep on swingin' at 'em!"[1]

I can just imagine that the fans cheered when Babe hit a home run, but it is likely that they didn't cheer when he struck out. It is the nature of people to cheer only when we are giving them what they want, but I believe Jesus is still cheering for us when we strike out in life. Why? Not because He is glad that we made a mistake, but simply because He knows that if He cheers when we are down, His encouragement will help us get back up. He is with us for the long haul in life and not merely for the times when we hit home runs. Isn't it comforting and empowering to know that God loves you just as much when you strike out as He does when you hit a home run? I know it is to me.

Every day won't be a home-run day for us, but we can be secure in the knowledge that God loves us with a perfect and everlasting love.

I have noticed among people who are great sports fans how much they love and cheer for their favorite players when they are doing well, and how quickly they begin to criticize when the players get into a slump and don't perform well for a period of time.

I am glad that when I am in a slump God cheers me on and tells me that I can have a comeback instead of rejecting me and leaving me alone, giving up on me. All of our days are not home-run days, but we will always come back and hit home runs again if we have the proper encouragement. If you cannot get the encouragement you need from people, then start listening to God because His Word is filled with one encouraging love letter after another written directly to you.

Acceptance Breeds Confidence

In my book titled *Confidence*, which is about the freedom to be yourself, I said, "A lack of confidence equals a lack of revelation concerning who you are in Christ." Although I wrote this book many years ago, I still feel the same way, only stronger than ever before. I found no heal-

> A lack of confidence equals a lack of revelation concerning who you are in Christ.

ing for my soul until I received love and right standing with God through faith in Jesus. As I did, I grew in confidence. Our confidence must be deeply rooted in Christ and His love and commitment to us. As we learn to feel good about ourselves and safe in our relationship with God, we are able to step out and do amazing things in life, even if we have to initially do them afraid. This is possible because we know it is permissible if we strike out occasionally, as long as we keep getting up to bat.

> *We keep going back, stronger, not weaker, because we will not allow rejection to beat us down. It will only strengthen our resolve. To be successful there is no other way.*
>
> Earl G. Graves (author and publisher)

I think that anyone who has experienced rejection and the feelings of being unwanted and then recovers is actually stronger than someone who has never experienced those feelings at all. Being knocked down in life and getting back up help us build a resolve that is vital for success. Author Paul Sweeney put it this way: "True success is overcoming the fear of being unsuccessful."[2]

Fear of rejection is a deep-rooted fear that affects many. When a person lives afraid that someone might disapprove of or reject them, this fear seeps into the very pores of who they are. They hesitate to trust others or engage in relationships because they doubt they will be accepted.

Past hurts keep many from opening up and living in freedom. Rather than dealing with the pain of the past and moving on in God, they rehearse the pain and live captive to a fear that it will happen again.

But the Bible gives great hope to the person who has been rejected and unwanted: Jesus understands that pain because He experienced it Himself. He understands the feelings that come when people push you away and make you feel devalued. Perhaps that is why Jesus used the final verse in the book of Matthew to tell His disciples:...*And behold, I am with you all the days (perpetually, uniformly, and on every occasion), to the [very] close and consummation of the age.*

In His final moments on Earth, Jesus wanted these men to know that they are never alone. Though others might reject them, though others might abandon them, He never would. Jesus would be with them in every situation, on every day, no matter what.

And just as Jesus was with the disciples, He is with you too. You need not fear the rejection of man because you have a friend in Jesus. You may have been turned away in the past. You may have suffered abuse and pain from those who were supposed to protect you. You may be hesitant to open your heart and be vulnerable again, but don't allow fear to rob you of the life Jesus came to give.

He accepts you! He delights in you! He is with you always!

Knowing that you have complete acceptance from Jesus will

give you confidence to do anything you need or want to do in life. You can live a free, full, and exciting life if you will refuse to settle for anything less. You have tremendous potential just waiting to be developed, but remember that you must be willing to strike out sometimes in order to hit home runs.

CHAPTER 12

The Fear of Being Inadequate

I can do all things through Christ who strengthens me.
Philippians 4:13 (NKJV)

Try to identify the historical figure from the following brief paragraph:

> When I was seven years old, my family was forced out of our home because of a legal technicality. I had to work to help support my family. At age nine, while still a backwards, shy little boy, my mother died. At age 22, I lost my job as a store clerk. I wanted to go to law school, but my education wasn't good enough. At 23, I went into debt to become a partner in a small store. Three years later my partner died leaving me a huge debt, which took years to repay. At 28, after developing romantic relations with a young lady for four years, I asked her to marry me. She said no. At 37, on my third try, I was finally elected to the United States Congress. Two years later, I ran again and failed to be re-elected. I had a nervous breakdown at that time. At 41, adding additional heartache to an already unhappy marriage, my four-year-old son died. The next year I ran for Land Officer and lost. At 45, I ran for the Senate and lost. A few years later, I ran for the Vice Presidency and lost. At 49, I ran for the Senate again and lost. And at 51, I was elected President of the United States.

Who am I?

My name is Abraham Lincoln.

Lincoln's life was one continuous failure. But he kept on going and became probably the greatest president in American history. He realized that failure is not final.[1]

I believe that Abraham Lincoln's legacy and impact on the world was only felt because he realized that failure is not final. Lincoln apparently did not feel inadequate even though he experienced a lot of rejection, and was unsuccessful quite often. Talk about someone who could have felt unwanted! If he would have felt inadequate, he certainly would have given up early in life and the world would have been robbed of the amazing gifts and talents he had. The example that Lincoln set is proof to me that no matter how often we strike out in life, if we keep getting up to bat, we will eventually hit a home run. He failed at many things and yet he was not an ultimate failure, and I am sure it was because he refused to feel defeated and inadequate. No one can know why he failed so many times before he experienced success, but his life is proof that we can succeed if we won't give up.

You Have What It Takes

Thoughts of inadequacy sound like this: *I am not capable, I don't think I have what it takes, I can't, I am not, I lack…*Those and other similar thoughts rob us of the vision and creativity to be the best that we can be. I have learned, through God's Word and my own experiences, that I can indeed do anything God wants me to do through Him. That literally means that He will give us the ability we need if we trust Him to do so. We cannot do things

> *If God wants us to do a thing, we can be assured that He will provide everything we need for the task.*

that are against God's will, but if God wants us to do a thing, we can be assured that He will provide everything we need for the task. Perhaps the next time you are trying to do something that you cannot seem to do, you should ask yourself if you are doing what God wants you to do, or merely what you want to do. If it is just your plan and it isn't working, then drop it, but if you are sure it is God's will for you, then don't give up!

I often hear people express fears about their inadequacy in various areas, but one I hear often is the fear of their inadequacy to be a good parent. They are so fearful of making mistakes that they cannot flow in the natural gifting that God gives us to be parents. Are there bad parents? Absolutely there are, but they are not people who are seeking to be good ones. If you truly want to be a good parent, you can relax because a lot of it is common sense. I was raised in a very dysfunctional home and can safely say that I did not have good parenting, yet I was a good mother to four children who all love God and are doing well in life. I prayed every night to be a good wife and a good mother and when we do that, it opens the door for God to help us. I wasn't a perfect parent by any means, and you won't be either, but you need not feel inadequate to parent. Actually, you should not feel inadequate to do anything that you need to do in life. We may be inadequate for many things without God's help, but in and through Him, we can do all things (see Philippians 4:13).

The fear that we are inadequate is just another way of saying that we are afraid of failure. The fear of inadequacy steals our confidence. Without confidence, we usually won't even try things, and even if we do, we are unsuccessful because at the core of our being we don't really believe we can do what we have set out to do. If we don't believe in our success, then who will? We cannot motivate other people to trust us if we don't trust ourselves. I know that in the back of many people's minds the nagging thought of *What if I fail?* is still lurking, but it's time to ignore that thought and listen to courage instead. Courage doesn't ask, "What if I fail?" Courage asks, "What if I succeed?"

Remember what the shepherd boy, David, asked when he heard Goliath spouting curses and insults against God and the armies of Israel? David, full of courage, asked, "What shall be done for the man who kills this Philistine and takes away the reproach from Israel?" (1 Samuel 17:26). While everyone else was thinking, *What if I fail?* David was thinking, *What If I succeed?*

It's important to note that most successes are not "overnight successes." I think it is safe to say that there are setbacks in nearly every venture. Things happen that we didn't expect, and some of them are arrows from Satan to make us believe that we are inadequate for the task at hand, or perhaps for any task at all. Very few people simply decide what they want to do and have immediate success, and even if they did, I am not sure it would be good for them. Usually we appreciate our successes more if we have to make a genuine investment in order to have them. I often say that my greatest testimony is simply, "I am still here." What I mean by that is that even though there have been many setbacks along my journey, I did not give up. With God's help, I kept getting up to bat and finally hit some home runs.

Failing Our Way to Success

"Failure is not an option" is a quote of many people with Type A personalities, but in reality, millions of people can't fail because they haven't even begun. They won't try anything, especially not anything out of the ordinary, due to the fear of being inadequate and failing. Their fear keeps them trapped in safe, narrow, boring, and frustrating lives. They have goals, hopes, and dreams that they will never realize because they don't want to fail.

Many times, the answer for progress is actually in failing. Michael Jordan's story is fascinating because he's one of the world's greatest basketball players of all time, yet he couldn't make the cut on his team in high school. Michael Jordan said, "I've missed more than 9,000 shots in my career. I've lost almost 300 games. Twenty-six times I've been trusted to take the game-winning shot and missed. I've failed over and over and over again in my life, and that is why I succeed."[2] You see, only those willing to keep on failing at times will also enjoy those times of success.

Thomas Edison said, "I failed my way to success."[3] Henry Ford said, "One who fears failure limits his activities. Failure is only the opportunity to more intelligently begin again."[4] John Maxwell wrote an entire book that teaches people how to "fail forward." Thinking like this will prevent failure from being permanent.

One very well known worship leader that I know failed music class. I barely passed English class and have written 100-plus books and have a daily television program sharing the Gospel with people around the world.

I read about two singers and how their reaction to the symptoms of nervousness before going onstage affected them completely differently. One of them wanted to completely back out, and for the other one, it was a signal that it's "Showtime!" I have preached thousands of times; yet I often look at my notes and wonder if I will have enough to say. These types of feelings are not a problem unless we let them stop us. We must move past fear and "do it afraid."

Fear of Failure: Signs and Symptoms

The fear of failure, as with all fears, keeps us from enjoying some aspect of life. The fear of failure is often one of the most paralyzing fears. Sometimes we are so concerned about failing that we don't try an activity we want to try, and we can end up resenting other people who are enjoying their lives while we sit on the sidelines and watch. Other times our fear of failure is so strong that we subconsciously undermine our own efforts so we don't have to continue to try. The fear is so strong that it brings about the defeat that we feared.

The fear of failure is usually caused by some traumatic event in early life, like demeaning parents or siblings, or teachers. It can also be caused by some event that caused great embarrassment. It doesn't help that our culture demands so much perfection. Perfection is an illusion, but people with crippling phobias won't try anything until they feel that their perfection is guaranteed, something none of us can have. The only way to know if we can ever do a thing is to try to do it and see. Step out and find out! Even a turtle can't get anywhere unless he sticks his neck out.

> *The only way to know if we can ever do a thing is to try to do it and see. Step out and find out!*

If you step out and try, you might not end up with perfection, but it is better than being stuck doing nothing.

Anxiety is a symptom of fear. Someone said that anxiety is fear's first cousin and that we can define anxiety as experiencing failure in advance. Anxiety steals our "now life" because mentally and emotionally, we are looking ahead thinking that there will be a negative result of some kind. Thinking that I might lose my job steals the joy of having one. Being afraid of illness causes stress and steals our health. Being anxious about our ability to parent properly prevents us from receiving wisdom from God to do so. Fear of any kind has no positive results. It steals everything good that God wants for us and prevents us from enjoying anything we do have.

I encourage you to expect something good to happen instead of being anxious that it won't. When we work with anticipation, it is more fun and can often be a self-fulfilling point of view. God is good and He wants us to expect Him to be good to us (see Isaiah 30:18). God is waiting to help us with everything we need to do in life. All He wants is to be invited to help us. The truth is that most of us are very inadequate without God's help, but through Christ we can do whatever we need to do in life.

Have you ever met anyone who always has a little sarcastic or negative comment to make about people who are successful? I have, and I always assumed it was jealousy. I am sure that jealousy does play into the problem, but I also have come to think that if a person has the need to diminish someone else's success with negative comments, it may be due to their own fears. Perhaps they have been afraid of failure, and their resentment of those who are succeeding is merely a symptom of that fear. People who make these comments might say things like, "I would be successful too if I had been born with a silver spoon in my mouth." Or, "He isn't all that talented, he was just lucky." Comments like these are merely proof that we resent the success of others, and there is no reason to resent it if we have done all we can do to have successes of our own. I often say, "Don't be jealous of what someone else has if you don't want to do what they did to get it."

What Do You Believe About Yourself?

I urge people to stop and take an inventory of how they feel about themselves. A lot of our problems are that we don't feel very good about ourselves. God assigns value to us and He equips us with gifts, abilities, and talents, and we need to believe that with God all things are possible. Inadequate feelings often come from comparing ourselves with someone else, but God isn't asking us to be anyone other than our own unique self. I may not be able to do what someone else can do, but I can do what I can do, and it is often something that nobody else can do. Do you feel small, minimized, or just plain incapable? If so, you are not the first one to feel that way.

Many of the people we call Bible heroes had to face the same feelings of inadequacy that we do. Moses felt inadequate for the job God was calling him to. He actually told God that He had the wrong man and needed to give the job to someone else. Moses said, "Who am I, that I should go to Pharaoh and bring the Israelites out of Egypt?" (Exodus 3:11). Perhaps many of us have asked that question when great opportunity was in front of us. People might even say to us, "Who do you think you are?" and understandably so because God often calls us to do things that we are not naturally qualified for.

God answered Moses' concern by simply saying, "I will surely be with you" (Exodus 3:12). The same reason He gives in answer regarding all fear. "Fear not for I am with you." All Moses had to do was take the first step of faith, and then as he experienced the faithfulness of God, it enabled him to take another and another until he had completed the task.

Zacchaeus was a little man who was so short that he could not see Jesus over the crowd of people. He could have felt inadequate, but he was aggressive and climbed a tree and ended up with the best view of anyone. Jesus also noticed his tenacity and decided to go to his house for dinner.

Paul was perhaps the greatest of all the apostles and his name meant *small* and *little*. I would rather have a name that meant *strong* and *great*, wouldn't you? But neither Paul's name, nor the mistakes he had made in life, kept him from becoming a great man.

These three examples are of people who had reason to feel inadequate but refused to do so. They pressed past their concerns and fears, but there are other examples in God's Word of those who didn't.

Twelve men were sent into the Promised Land as spies and were to bring back a report. Ten came back and stated that although the land was very good, there were giants in the land and they were afraid to go in. They made this statement: "We were in our own sight as grasshoppers, and so we were in their sight" (Numbers 13:33). People see us the way we see ourselves. They felt inadequate, and the giants realized it. There was no point in them fighting—they had lost the fight before it ever began due to their fears.

Only two of the spies gave a good report saying, "We are well able to conquer so let us go up at once" (Numbers 13:30). These two were Joshua and Caleb, and they had a different spirit from those who were fearful. They both went on to do great and mighty things, but we never hear of the 10 spies again who saw themselves as grasshoppers.

How do you see yourself? It is said that our self-image is like a photo we carry of ourselves. Take time to stop and reflect on how you think of yourself because a lot of other things in your life will be determined by those thoughts.

Is Your Life on Hold?

A fear of inadequacy and failure can put your life on hold. It causes you to avoid anything that you don't view as totally safe or a guaranteed success. We would all like guarantees that the choices we make will have good results, but that is not often the case. "If I change my hair color, will I like it?" "If I apply for a promotion at work, will I get it?" "If I get married, can I be guaranteed I will be happy?" I think that if we did have those guarantees it would take all the mystery out of life and we would feel safe, but bored! Much of what God offers us is a mystery. Faith is a mystery simply because it is based on something we cannot always see or feel.

We can see stepping out in faith as exciting or frightening; the choice is ours. I feel that my journey with God is exciting because I don't live in the fear of making a mistake.

> We can see stepping out in faith as exciting or frightening; the choice is ours.

Someone called me one morning and said, "I am going to ask you something that is really far out and a bit crazy," and I must admit, I thought, *Oh my, what is this all about!?* They even expressed again what a crazy idea they were about to present to me, which really made me curious. After the person told me what they wanted to ask me, I realized I was unable to grant their request, but I didn't look down on them for asking. I was even able to suggest someone else they might ask who could perhaps grant their request. The person could have been too frightened to ask, but their boldness may yet bear good fruit. Sometimes we have to start moving in order to figure out the direction we should take. When you step out and find that your direction is not correct, don't give up—just take a step in another direction and don't give up until you find the right one.

In my opinion people give up far too easily, and I would love to see people be a lot more persistent because I believe that persistence pays off. Get your life off of "hold." Get it out of park and start driving. Passivity is the devil's playground. He loves it when we shrink back in fear and do absolutely nothing. He loves it, but we don't. We may think we are safe, but actually we end up miserable. God has created us for progress, movement, mystery, and having goals and reaching them. We are cheating ourselves if we don't boldly go for all God has in mind for us.

Can't, Didn't, and Don't

Don't focus on what you can't do, what you didn't do, and what you don't do, but instead focus on what you can do, what you have done, and what you are doing. We absolutely must see ourselves, and our lives, in a positive way. Thinking too much about what you didn't do in the past and how things didn't work out will simply prevent you from trying again. Purpose to focus on one thing that you have been successful at and that will energize you to try something else. You do have potential, you are not inadequate, you are capable, and you will be robbing the rest of us if you won't believe it!

Perhaps your experience with yourself in the past hasn't been one of success, but I always say, "It isn't over until it's over, and it's not over yet."

> It isn't over until it's over, and it's not over yet.

Maybe you feel that life has thrown you under the bus, but you can still decide to get up and drive the bus if you want to. It is never too late for a new beginning in how you approach life. If you have been fearful in the past, or have felt inadequate, today is the best day for a change! Let this be the day that you begin to "do it afraid"!

CHAPTER 13

I Am Afraid I Am Not Doing Enough

…What are we to do, that we may [habitually] be working the works of God? [What are we to do to carry out what God requires?]

John 6:28

As long as we believe we must do something to be accepted by God, we will always wonder if we are doing enough. "What do I need to do?" seems to be one of our most frequent prayer concerns. It is the same question that the crowd asked Jesus, as recorded in the Scripture verse above.

A survey of our ministry employees revealed the same concern. The number one question that they said they would like to ask Jesus was, "How can I tell when I am doing enough?" I am not surprised by the survey because that was my biggest question for many long years. I may not have formed my fear into a question all the time, but the wondering rolled around and around in my thinking. *Am I doing enough? Did I pray long enough? Am I doing enough good works to please God? Did I watch too much television yesterday, or should I have spent that time working?* I wanted to know the same thing the crowd wanted to know, and the same thing that many of you want to know..."Is God pleased?" "Am I doing enough?" "Is God pleased with me or is He disappointed and perhaps even angry with me?"

This fear is perhaps one of the most tormenting that we experience because it never lets us rest or relax. We constantly feel we need to be doing something else and yet we often don't know what to do. We are afraid that God is not pleased, and the fear is birthed in not truly knowing the character of God, or the plan of salvation carried out in Jesus Christ.

Let's imagine that a man and woman have four children, and each morning the children run to their parents and say, "What can we do for you today in order to get you to accept us?" How would that make the parents feel? If I were that parent I would think, "What am I doing wrong that causes my children to believe they need to buy my love with good works?" If, on the other hand, they came to me and said, "Mom, we love you so much that we want to do something for you today; what can we do to bless you?" That would make me feel so good I would jump up and down and clap my hands! Wow! I would feel appreciated, valued, and honored, and so would any of you who are parents. I want my children to bless me because they love me, not because they are afraid of me.

We Can Never Do Enough

The truth is that we can never do enough for God no matter how much we do! I know that sounds frustrating and defeating, but it is good news when we realize that Jesus has done all that needs to be done and nothing we can ever do will improve on the job He did. True rest comes when we can say, "I don't have

> *Jesus has done all that needs to be done and nothing we can ever do will improve on the job He did.*

to do anything to get God to love and accept me." No matter how good we are, we are never good enough to meet God's standard without Jesus. We must present to God all that Jesus is and realize that we stand before God "in Christ," and not in ourselves. We have access to the throne of God's grace because of the blood of Christ, and not because of anything we can ever do.

> *In Whom, because of our faith in Him, we dare to have the boldness (courage and confidence) of free access (an unreserved approach to God with freedom and without fear).*
>
> Ephesians 3:12

Take a moment and grasp the beautiful meaning of this Scripture. We can come before God "boldly" and "without fear" because of our faith in Him, not because we have struggled and agonized long enough to be able to say, "I have finally done enough."

When we pray in Jesus' name, we are presenting to the Father all that Jesus is, not what we are. That is why we pray in His name, and not in our own.

> *And I will do [I myself will grant] whatever you ask in My Name [as presenting all that I Am], so that the Father may be glorified and extolled in (through) the Son.*
>
> *[Yes] I will grant [I Myself will do for you] whatever you shall ask in My Name [as presenting all that I Am].*
>
> John 14:13–14

We Want to Rest

We have a desire to rest, not just physically but spiritually, mentally, and emotionally. We have a deep need and desire to enter what Scripture calls "the rest of God." Jesus said that if we come to Him, He will give us rest for our souls (see Matthew 11:28). The apostle Paul teaches us that we can enter the rest of God if we believe (see Hebrews 4:3).

We want to rest from the agonizing fear that we have not done enough, which then leads to pushing ourselves to try to do more, and more, and more. Let us make a decision to believe God's Word, and the moment we do, then and only then can we rest from the weariness of our own works.

Our approval has been purchased with the blood sacrifice of Jesus Christ. We are bought and paid for and now belong to God! He is pleased if we simply believe in what Jesus did for us!

> Jesus replied, This is the work (service) that God asks of you: that you believe in the One Whom He has sent [that you cleave to, trust, rely on, and have faith in His Messenger].
>
> John 6:29

Jesus answered the crowd with the words recorded above and His answer still applies to us who have the same question they did. You can relax because the requirements of God have all been met in Jesus.

You can relax because the requirements of God have all been met in Jesus.

I know that it sounds too good to be true, and you may be afraid to believe that you no longer need to be afraid that you're not doing enough, but I promise you that it is true!

A Pure Heart

There are things that God wants us to do. He has called us to bear good fruit, and the apostle John tells us that God is glorified when we bear much, abundant fruit (see John 15:8). But our motive for doing the work is what God is truly interested in. If our motive (the reason why we are doing the work) is not according to the will of God, then the work is rejected as a counterfeit and we lose all the reward connected to the deed (see 1 Corinthians 3:13–15).

Our works must be done out of faith and not out of fear. They must be done to give something to God, not to get something from Him. This would be an excellent time to stop and ask yourself why you are doing the various things you do. I love doing what I call "motive checks." It is very easy for us to deceive ourselves about our motives, so it is good to take the time occasionally to ask God to show you anything that you might be doing for a wrong reason.

We should not do what we do in order to gain approval from God, but we should do these things because we love Him. We must not do good works to be seen of men, or to be applauded, admired, or well thought of. In order for a work to be pure it must meet the following qualifications.

1. Work done for God must be done purely because we love Him.
2. Work done for God must be done in obedience to Him and His Word.
3. Work done for God must be done by faith, leaning entirely on Him and trusting in Him for the success of the work.
4. Work done for God must be done to glorify Him.

5. Work done for God should not be done for acknowledg-
ment, admiration, or applause by people.

God's eyes roam around the earth searching for someone
whose heart is pure before Him (see 2 Chronicles 16:9). A pure
heart is much more important to the
Lord than a perfect record of good
works. Although it isn't possible to
have perfection in all of our behavior, it is totally possible to have a perfect heart toward God. A person with
a perfect heart would be someone who deeply desires to please
God in all things, and is always open to growth and change that
is motivated and led by the Holy Spirit.

> A pure heart is much more important to the Lord than a perfect record of good works.

In Matthew 5:48 we are admonished "be perfect," but the
meaning of the phrase is to grow into complete maturity in godli-
ness in mind and character. Spiritually, I am growing all the time,
but I have not arrived at perfection yet, and neither has any other
human for that matter. The apostle Paul stated that he pressed
toward the mark of perfection, but that he had not arrived (see
Philippians 3:11–13).

Don't live in the fear that you have not done enough and that
God is angry with you, or that the door to His presence is closed
to you. I can assure you that if you truly believe in Jesus and the
work He did on your behalf, you are doing enough.

As mentioned previously, it is definitely God's desire that we
do good works. James said that faith without works is dead, and I
totally agree, but works that are done without faith are also dead.
Have true faith in God and His promises first and then the works
will follow, but they will be pure works done from a pure heart.
It is quite impossible to have a genuine relationship with God

through Christ and not deeply desire to please God. Once we realize what Jesus has done for us, we will love Him so much that doing things for Him and His glory becomes our motivation for living.

Relax and look to the work Jesus did on your behalf, and always remember that the work you do does not buy your acceptance with God. Acceptance has already been purchased with the blood of Christ. The work we do is our way of saying "Thank You" to our amazing God, who loves us so much He sent His only Son to redeem us from our sin and has seated us in heavenly places with Christ.

> For God so loved the world, that He gave his only begotten Son, that whosoever believeth in Him, should not perish, but have everlasting life.
>
> John 3:16 (KJV)

CHAPTER 14

The Fear of Man

So we take comfort and are encouraged and confidently and boldly say, The Lord is my Helper; I will not be seized with alarm [I will not fear or dread or be terrified]. What can man do to me?

Hebrews 13:6

When we approach the subject of fear, many things come to mind: a fear of failure, a fear of danger or harm to ourselves or those we love, the fear of losing what we have, fear that we are not doing enough to please God, and so on. But if there is one fear that stands above all the others, casting the longest shadow, it is perhaps the fear of man.

The fear of man for many people is an ever-present and addictive fear that attempts to maximize the position of man and minimize the power of God. The fear of man is the result of setting others, their opinions of us, and their importance or their perceived power above God.

Solomon said it this way . . .

The fear of man brings a snare, but whoever leans on, trusts in, and puts his confidence in the Lord is safe and set on high.

Proverbs 29:25

In this one verse, Israel's wisest king gives us both the risk and the reward. The fear of man is a snare—a trap. It will encage us if we allow it to. We risk our freedom when we fear man; however, we don't have to fall prey to its deception. When we lean on, trust in, and put our confidence in the Lord, we will experience the reward of not fearing man and we will be safe and set on high.

A story from my own life explains how the fear of man takes away our freedom to be ourselves and make our own decisions:

Due to insecurities that developed in my childhood and a desperate need for friends and acceptance, I fell into the trap of saying and doing what I thought others wanted me to instead of being truthful. There existed a certain group within the church that my husband, my children, and I attended that would have been considered to be the "elite" group, the group most sought after to be part of. These church members controlled a lot of the decisions made at the church, and they more or less decided who was in their group and who was not. Groups like this exist in most places, and sadly, the church is usually not exempt from them. They are in schools, neighborhoods, governments, where we work, and yes, in the church.

I worked very hard to be part of this group and to be friends with one woman in particular who wielded a lot of power within the group. I knew that if I could gain her friendship and acceptance, that I could be part of the "in crowd." In order to gain her approval, I had to do everything she wanted, and I do mean everything! I finally gained her acceptance but quickly found that I had to keep it the same way I gained it. After a short while I realized I was in a trap and had given up my right to be myself. Interestingly enough, getting out of a relationship like that is often harder than getting in. It cannot be done without an explosion of some sort, and that meant a lot of people would know and probably blame me. Since we often cannot face the thought of the possible fallout, we stay in bondage; I did.

It is possible that you have experienced the same type of relationship I am describing, or it is even possible that you are currently in one. It will take great courage to break free, especially if that relationship has become a habitual pattern in your life.

I know you want to know the end of my story, so I will finish it before I go on. As I became increasingly tired of being controlled and found myself wanting to escape, I had to consider the benefits she afforded me and ask myself if I was willing to lose them. You see, I got invited to all the right parties, I was privy to all kinds of secrets about lots of people at the church, and had the distinction of being her "best friend." Letting her control me gained me acceptance from others, and I had to decide if I was willing to give it all up.

As I was pondering how to handle this situation, I had a life-changing encounter with God. He touched my life in a very profound way and called me to teach His Word. I was excited, to say the least, but quickly discovered that my so-called friends were not excited. They felt that I had become too religious and was being deceived, and they made it clear that if I pursued the course I felt God had placed in front of me, I would be out of the group and no longer welcome at the church. Eventually, the elders of the church, many of whom were part of the group along with the pastor, gathered with Dave and me and asked us to leave the church because, in their opinion, I was deceived and being rebellious.

Wow! "Painful" doesn't even begin to describe what I went through. I have since come to appreciate that painful part of my life. God revealed to me that these people were not ever true friends, and He saved me from further pain by arranging for my exit. I didn't have to decide to leave…I was thrown out! Not a great way to start a ministry!

I wish I could say that I learned my lesson and never repeated the mistake again, but I did repeat it on at least two other occasions that I can recall. The same thing happened at the next church I went to. I was in leadership in that church, and by then I was teaching God's Word and I finally felt valuable, but once again I allowed myself to be controlled by people in order to gain and maintain the position I had, as well as the acceptance of certain people. I had an important position, and it gained me admiration, but I paid a high price for it.

Don't Say "Yes" When Your Heart Screams "No"

Have you ever had a boss at work who required more out of you than was right and fair, but you were afraid to speak up? Have you ever been part of a group of people who made it clear that you would be "out" if you didn't do as they wanted? Have you ever had someone in your life who was a controller and a manipulator, and you knew deep down inside of you that you needed to stand up to that person and yet you didn't? Have you felt peer pressure? Most of us have at some time, but the people who have serious problems with the fear of man are usually wounded, fearful, insecure people who have experienced rejection and don't want to experience it again. The pain of rejection is intense, and most of us will do just about anything to avoid it.

> *The pain of rejection is intense, and most of us will do just about anything to avoid it.*

Although none of us wants to be rejected, it is very important that we follow God rather than man. There are times when we can please both God and man, but that is not always the case. When we have to choose, we should always choose God. When we don't obey God in order to please people, we lose our peace and end up experiencing condemnation. Nothing feels quite as bad as knowing we shouldn't do something but doing it anyway.

I recall how I felt during those years when I said "yes" to people even though my heart was screaming "no." I felt guilty, pressured, and even angry that I was letting myself be controlled. I made excuses for my behavior that deceived me into thinking I was doing the right thing, but deep inside I knew I wasn't. For example, I told myself that I was simply being easy to get along with, keeping the peace, or adapting to others. All of these can be good and are things the Word of God encourages us to do, but not at the cost of not walking in wisdom or disobeying God.

Most of us have heard the phrase, "Don't be a 'yes' man." Don't be the kind of person who does what everyone else wants you to do all the time, at the cost of losing your own identity and freedom. And if you are in that trap right now in your life, then it is time to break free and start being true to your own heart even if you have to do it afraid. Let me remind you that fear cannot be conquered any way other than facing it and doing what you should do, even if you have to do it afraid.

The apostle Paul assured those that he ministered to that they could depend on him to be trustworthy and faithful in all of his speech. We should make a commitment to be the same way. Don't be two-faced! Be the kind of person who says what you mean, and means what you say.

> *As surely as God is trustworthy and faithful and means what He says, our speech and message to you have not been Yes [that might mean] No.*
>
> 2 Corinthians 1:18

The people could depend on Paul to be truthful and honest with them, and I believe that is the basis for all truly good and healthy relationships. Not only should we be truthful with others, but we should also give them permission to be truthful with us. Don't ever try to force people to do what you want them to do, but instead encourage them to follow their heart.

Jesus dealt with the importance of being truthful when He said...

> *Let your Yes be simply Yes, and your No be simply No; anything more than that comes from the evil one.*
>
> Matthew 5:37

God certainly never leads us to be people-pleasers or to be ensnared in the fear of man. He never leads us to say "yes" to people when we know in our heart we should say "no." Nor does He lead us to say "no" when we know we should say "yes." Being honest with ourselves and others is vital to our spiritual growth and freedom.

We might keep a job by always telling the boss what he or she wants to hear instead of being honest, but we will be miserable! We might keep our friends by always telling them what they want to hear, but we will be miserable! Jesus did not die for us so we could be miserable; He died so we could be free!

The Fear of Man Keeps Us from Our Destiny

I don't think it's an exaggeration to say that more people don't fulfill their destiny than those who do, and the fear of man is one of the root causes.

In order to do what God is leading us to do, we often have to be misunderstood or possibly even rejected by people. Jesus came to do the will of His Father in Heaven and to help mankind, yet He was rejected. Doing the right thing doesn't always guarantee acceptance from people.

At some point in life, every person must decide whether they will be a "people-pleaser" or a "God-pleaser." Our goal should be to please God no matter what the cost. It may cost us our reputation to walk away from something we don't want to give up,

> *At some point in life, every person must decide whether they will be a "people-pleaser" or a "God-pleaser."*

or to do something we don't want to do, but the rewards are always worth the sacrifice in the end.

Jesus had to lose His reputation to do the will of God, but His reputation today is excellent all around the world. I lost my reputation with my little group of so-called friends at church in order to do the will of God, and for a while I was lonely, but God has replaced those people who rejected me with many genuine friends and a better reputation than those former friends could have ever given me.

The apostle Paul said that if he had been trying to be popular with people, he would have never become an apostle (see Galatians 1:10). He followed God and fulfilled his destiny. There are others mentioned in the Bible who wanted to follow Jesus because they did believe in Him, but they would not for fear of being expelled from the synagogue (see John 12:41–43). They missed their destiny because they wanted to be loved and admired by people.

> *For they loved the approval and the praise and the glory that come from men [instead of and] more than the glory that*

comes from God. [They valued their credit with men more
than their credit with God.]

John 12:43

When I read this Scripture, it makes me sad to think of all the
people who have missed their destiny for the same reason. They
valued their reputation with men more than with God. When we
are faced with these types of challenges in life, we should seriously consider the consequences of making the wrong choice.
As most of us know, human beings are quite fickle and ever-
changing in their commitments, so it is foolish indeed to let our
fear of them rule us.

If you have made mistakes in the past, please remember and
believe that it is never too late to begin again. A few right choices
can often undo the results of a bad one. Anyone who is breathing
has an opportunity to have a great life still. All they have to do is
immediately start following God rather than people.

The Fear of What People Think

The fear of man is often merely the fear of what they think of
us, but in reality what can a thought that someone else has do to
us? Is it pride that makes us overly concerned with what people
think? I believe it is! It is not what they think that we fear, but
what they think of US! It is all about us.

The simple definition of pride is "I." I want. I think. I feel. I
need. Pride is defined in the *Vine's Greek Dictionary* as *being high-
minded, or thinking more highly of oneself than one ought to.* Our
concern about what people think of us is usually excessive, and
it creates fear and turns us into people-pleasers. Our pride must
be dealt with before this fear can be eradicated! It hurts our pride

to consider that someone may think or say something critical about us, but it won't defeat us if we truly know who we are in Christ and how much He loves and cares for us. God says many good things about us in His Word, so we shouldn't be worried about the people who criticize us.

My husband is a very secure man and he really doesn't care what people think of him. He always says, "If I am doing what I believe in my heart to be right and someone thinks badly of me, that is not my problem; it is between them and God."

Being excessively concerned about what others think is a total waste of time because we cannot completely control what they think anyway. Certainly it is enjoyable to have a good reputation, and everyone wants to be well thought of; however, we must not become man-pleasers in order to get somewhere.

> Being excessively concerned about what others think is a total waste of time because we cannot completely control what they think anyway.

No matter what we do, someone won't like it and someone will think something of us other than what we would like for them to, so why let it control us? The psalmist David said, "I will not fear. What can man do to me?" (Psalm 118:6). And the writer of Hebrews quoted David in Hebrews 13:6 by repeating the same thing: "I will not fear. What can man do to me?" We need to say the same thing daily, or perhaps several times a day. Let's be practical about this and ponder the question, "What can man really do to me?" Perhaps they can reject us, prevent us from getting something we want, or hurt our feelings, but what they can do to us is minor when compared to what God can do for us as we walk in obedience to Him.

Even if a person is successful in taking something away from us, God will return it in better condition than it was when we lost it. I lost my reputation, but it is better now than it was when I lost it. I lost my friends, but I have more now than I did then—genuine friends at that. To have the glory that God desires for us, we may go through a season of suffering, but that suffering brings us into the best God has for us. If we put God first in all of our concerns, we will always do well in life. Seek first the kingdom of God and His righteousness and all of the things you need will be added (see Matthew 6:33).

> *Of all the memorials in Westminster Abbey, there is not one that gives a nobler thought than that inscribed on the monument to Lord Lawrence—simply his name, with the date of his death, and these words: "He feared man so little, because he feared God so much."*[1]

When our fear of displeasing God is greater than our fear of displeasing man, we will overcome the fear of man.

The Fear of Sharing Our Faith with Others

Part of the teaching of Christianity is that we should share our faith with others in the hopes of leading them to a relationship with Christ. Many people are afraid to do this because they are concerned about what others will think of them.

Norman Cates shared the humorous story of a Christian guy who prayed this prayer every morning: "Lord, if You want me to witness to someone today, please give me a sign to show me who it is." One day he found himself on a bus when a big, burly man sat next to him; the big guy burst into tears and began to weep. He then cried out with a loud voice, "I need to be saved. I'm a lost sinner and I need the Lord. Won't somebody tell me how to be saved?" He turned to the Christian and pleaded, "Can you show me how to be saved?" The believer immediately bowed his head and prayed, "Lord, is this a sign?"

A humorous story indeed, but for some of us it might take an event like this to get us to share our faith. The fear of being rejected or thought poorly of often stops us from sharing our faith in Christ. We don't need to cram the Gospel down the throat of those who have no interest, but we should be bold enough to share when it is obvious God is opening the door or when people tell us they are hurting and need answers to their problems. Jesus is the answer to the problems in the world, and it is easy to share about Him if we are not immobilized by the fear of what people think of us.

I attended a particular church when I was a very young woman desiring to be in ministry, and this church placed a strong emphasis on witnessing for Christ. They urged people to hand out Gospel tracts everywhere they went. I did it although I wasn't comfortable doing it, and eventually I got to the point where I didn't even want to go out because I felt I had to share with everyone I came in contact with. I had made a law out of sharing my faith instead of trusting God to give me grace to do it when it was the right time and for the right person.

It is pointless to try to make someone eat if they are not hungry, and it is equally pointless to try to tell someone they need Jesus in their life if they don't think they need anything, let alone Jesus. By pushing people or seeming fanatical we can even make them more determined that a Christian is something they don't want to be.

I have learned to let God put me in the right place at the right time and to open the door for me to share my faith. Sometimes that door opens very quickly, but at other times I have been around someone for as long as a few years before the right time comes to talk to them. But in the meantime, I still witness with my life example. Eventually people become curious or they have a need in their life that provokes them to be open to talking to me. Once their heart is open and has been prepared by God, the rest is easy. While I am waiting for the right time, I might offer them a book or a Bible. I never try to hide my faith, and neither should you. Pray for God to give you opportunity, and when the door is open, go in boldly and don't let the fear of what the person will think stop you.

I talk about God naturally all the time because my relationship with Him is part of my life and it is not something I try to hide. For example, I frequently tell people that I will pray for them, or I might say in response to them sharing a problem, "Why don't you ask God to help you with that?" Sometimes I don't even get a response, but I am planting little seeds in the belief that, eventually, those seeds will take hold in people's hearts.

Jesus told His disciples that He would make them fishers of men (see Matthew 4:19), so I might say I think we should always be fishing for souls, but we cannot reel them in if they don't take the bait. Relax and trust God to lead you when it comes to witnessing about your faith in Christ to others.

The Fear of Man Offends God

If you promised your child that you would take care of him and yet he persisted in being afraid of the next-door neighbor, it might eventually be offensive to you. You expect your child to trust you and to know that you wouldn't let any harm come to him.

God feels the same way about us, so let's consider this Scripture:

The Lord of hosts—regard Him as holy and honor His holy name [by regarding Him as your only hope of safety], and let Him be your fear and let Him be your dread [lest you offend Him by your fear of man and distrust of Him].

Isaiah 8:13

God is good and He always has our best interests in mind. He promises to take care of us if we trust Him to do so. You will see God's promises fulfilled in your life when you step out on them. Believe in your heart and confess with your mouth that you trust God to take care of you and that you will not fear what man can do to you. As I have said over and over in this book, you may feel fear, but you don't have to let the feeling control your actions or decisions. Feel the fear and do what you know you should do anyway.

God is for you, and if He is for you, then it makes no difference who is against you! Don't let man be large in your eyes and God small. God is

> *God is for you, and if He is for you, then it makes no difference who is against you!*

greater than all men put together millions of times over. He created all that we see in this universe with a word, and surely He can take care of us.

Remember what we said at the beginning of this chapter: The fear of man brings a snare, it will entrap and torment you, but whoever leans on, trusts in, and puts his confidence in the Lord is safe and set on high (see Proverbs 29:25).

CHAPTER 15

The Fear of the Unknown

We all have a fear of the unknown, what one does with that fear will make all the difference in the world.

Lillian Russell

The fear of the unknown is a frequent fear that people deal with. The phone rings and a family member says, "I need to talk to you about something very important. Can you meet me next week to discuss it?" You try to get a bit of information out of the caller, but the person is determined to see you face-to-face. Now you have a week to wait for the "unknown" conversation to happen. Is this relative angry about something? Is there a problem in the family you don't know about? Is someone going to try to borrow money from you?

What you do with the fear will determine the quality of the week in front of you. You can trade the fear for trust in God, or you can keep reasoning, revolving your mind around and around an imaginary problem until you become anxious and lose a few nights of sleep.

Have you ever noticed that when things like that happen, we rarely imagine all kinds of wonderful things? Why not think, *I wonder if my relative is going to give me that extra car?* Or, *I wonder if my loved one is going to make me a wealthy heir?* Fear always shows up in a negative way, but faith is always positive. In a situation like the one

> Fear always shows up in a negative way, but faith is always positive.

above, we can refuse the fear and replace it with faith in God. We can believe that whatever the news is going to be, we will have the grace to handle the situation at the time. God does not promise us a trouble-free life, but He does promise to be with us at all times and to give us the strength and wisdom we need for coping with any trouble that comes our way.

There is probably more in life that we don't know than that we do, if you really stop to think about it. We don't know when or exactly how we will die. We don't know what the world economy will be like five years from now, or what the stock market will do next week. We don't know what kinds of choices our children will make. We don't know what might be going on inside of our bodies that we are not aware of. We don't know if we will get the promotion at work we so desperately want, and on and on the story goes.

There is so much that we don't know, but we can learn not to be anxious and worried about it. Worry is mentally prying into things that only God has answers for. If we knew everything God knew, we would not need to trust Him, and since our entire relationship with Him is based on faith, it is doubtful we will ever be without some unanswered questions. We will have to get comfortable with the unknown if we ever want to enjoy peace.

Although we all say we would like to know everything, I doubt seriously that we would. First, we would all find out some disturbing things that we would wish afterward we never discovered. Second, the mystery of life is what keeps it interesting. It would be very boring indeed if there were no surprises awaiting us in life.

Mystery

We might say that life is a mystery unfolding. As teenagers we look into the future and often we see nothing. Everyone wants to know what we want to do when we grow up, and we literally have no idea. We have to walk it out and find out for ourselves. I still marvel at the various things I did in life before I finally got to the specific thing my life was intended to be about.

I was an abused child and teenager, an office clerk, a book-keeper, a waitress, married at 19, abandoned in New Mexico and California, and ultimately divorced at 23, a single mother of one son. I was an office manager, a credit manager, married again at age 23 (I didn't wait long to try again), I had 2 more children, was a stay-at-home mom, then more jobs, mostly office work, and suddenly to my great surprise, called by God to be a minister and Bible teacher. Wow! Surprise! Where did that come from?

Nothing else I had done in life was even remotely anything like what I was about to do, although I did learn something in each phase that helped with the next one. But, to my great surprise, here I am today with an international television show broadcast in 70-plus languages, the author of 100-plus books, the mother of four children, and a wife of 48 years. If I had known what God had in mind, I am fairly certain I would have messed it up, or definitely tried to do it earlier than I should have.

As you can see from my story, surprises in life can be wonderful, but we often fail to realize it in time to enjoy life while we are waiting for them. I am a great advocate of enjoying every phase of life. I wish I had done so myself, but since I cannot go back and do my life over, at least I can encourage others not to waste the seasons and phases of their lives. We are all headed somewhere all of the time, so let's look forward to the future with happy anticipation instead of tormenting fear.

> We are all headed somewhere all of the time, so let's look forward to the future with happy anticipation instead of tormenting fear.

God is actually very fond of mystery. We can start with the mystery of our birth. The Bible says that we were formed "in secret" and in the region of "mystery" (our mom's womb) (see Psalm 139:15). Job said the dealings of God with the ungodly is a mystery (see Job 21:16). I am sure we can all say an "amen" to that. We wonder why the ungodly seem to prosper in the midst of their wicked ways, why they live so long, especially when a godly person we know dies young. We cannot figure out God simply because we wouldn't do things the way He does them.

In Mark 4:11, the kingdom of God is said to be a mystery. In Romans 16:25, as well as in several other verses, we are told that the entire plan of redemption is a mystery. Paul asked many times in prayer that he might be able to boldly proclaim the mystery of the Gospel that had been entrusted to him. After all, who could reasonably understand God sending His precious Son to die for sinners, and for that matter, why did He wait as long as He did to do it? We must grasp it with the heart, for the mind of man cannot understand the ways of God. God's plan and will is called a mystery (see Ephesians 1:9). The mystery of the ages is Christ in us, the hope of glory (see Colossians 1:27). Even lawlessness is referred to as a mystery (see 2 Thessalonians 2:7). Then there is the book of Revelation in the Bible, and it is one mystery after another!

As I sit here and write I have some sort of a plan for what I think my future may hold, but truthfully the whole thing is a mystery and only God knows for sure what will happen. Thankfully, I have come to a place of peace with that and trust God that whatever happens—whether I like it or I don't—He will be with me, and therefore, I need not fear . . . and neither do you.

I love the following statement by the apostle Paul:

> *For I resolved to know nothing (to be acquainted with nothing, to make a display of the knowledge of nothing, and to*

be conscious of nothing) among you except Jesus Christ (the Messiah) and Him crucified.

1 Corinthians 2:2

It seems to me that I can hear the passion in Paul's statement, and I think when he said it, he said it with an emphasis. It was as if he was completely finished with trying to understand everything and made a decision to know nothing but Christ!

I believe that knowing Him is the only way we can find peace with all of the unanswered questions in life. Paul was a scholar, and discovering the answers to things had been a large part of his life. He was highly educated, and at times people who are highly educated have to learn to embrace childlike faith. We know that God revealed Himself to Paul in a startling way, and one that could not be denied, but like all of us, Paul eventually had to trust without sight or understanding. I don't mean to say that we stop using our brain. God gave it to us and He does expect us to use it, but we cannot find God with it, because He is a mystery that cannot be understood with the finite mind. He can be grasped with the heart by faith. It is amazingly relaxing when we finally decide to simply believe, and to cease from having to understand.

Reasoning and Confusion

I was an expert at reasoning for most of my life until I was about 50 years old. That represents a lot of wasted and frustrating years. My mind roamed around and around trying to find answers to things that only God knew, and He wasn't telling anyone yet. God reveals things in His timing and not necessarily when we would like to know them. He withholds information purposely in order to train us to trust Him! As long as what we say we believe is just an idea, it doesn't amount to much. Only when what we believe is tested and tried do we discover the true value of our faith. We can say that we trust God all day long, but if we fear the unknown, then in reality, we don't trust God.

Joyfully, instead of trying to figure things out, we can trust God to reveal them at the right time. We are exhorted in God's Word to lean not to our own understanding, but in all of our ways to trust God with our mind and heart (see Proverbs 3:5–6). Go ahead and try it; you will start to enjoy life more than ever before.

Use some of the time you previously spent trying to figure things out seeking to know God better, and then you will have insight into secrets and mysteries also.

> [For I always pray to] the God of our Lord Jesus Christ, the Father of glory, that He may grant you a spirit of wisdom and revelation [of insight into mysteries and secrets] in the [deep and intimate] knowledge of Him.
>
> Ephesians 1:17

If we seek to know *things*, we may never know God as we should, but if we seek to know *Him*, we can be assured that He will show us everything we need to know at the exact right time.

Reasoning is not only a waste of time, but it is energy-draining. It is a work of the flesh, and works always drain us of energy and leave us frustrated. Nothing is worse than trying repeatedly to do something that we just simply cannot do.

> *If we seek to know things, we may never know God as we should, but if we seek to know Him, we can be assured that He will show us everything we need to know at the exact right time.*

Reasoning is also the root of confusion. It is impossible to become confused if we refuse to try to figure things out. We may certainly ponder a thing and pray for understanding, but excessive reasoning is quite another thing.

I have a guideline for myself that I will share with you. I do a lot of thinking, so in some ways I suppose we could say that I am a "mental" person. I have a lot of things that I have to think about, like the many messages I need to prepare for television programs and conferences, as well as books I write and interviews I do. However, when I think to the point where I start feeling confused, that is my signal that I have moved away from healthy thinking into ungodly reasoning that will lead to trouble for my soul. God is not the author of confusion (see 1 Corinthians 14:33), so when you feel confused, stop and ask yourself why you are. You will find that you are trying to figure something out you should just pray about and trust God to reveal at the right time.

You may feel afraid giving up the human instinct to "figure it out"; I know I did. I was really frightened to not have all of the answers, because then I felt out of control, and I didn't like that feeling. God had to teach me that even when I felt in control, I really wasn't, and that is true for all of us. Whatever we do manage to control, there are thousands of other things we are not in control of, and if God did not keep those things under control, everything in our life would be total chaos. The very thought of not having all the answers to everything was frightening to me, so I had to do it afraid in order to stop reasoning.

Each time I felt confused and knew that I was once again in an area I needed to not be in, I said, "I will trade this reasoning for trust," and I did it even though it frightened me and made me uncomfortable.

Recently someone told me they needed to meet with me face-to-face about some problem in an area of the ministry, but we could not meet for a couple of weeks. They requested that I not require them to give me any information before that meeting. After thinking about it way too long, I thought I knew what they wanted to meet about, and so I was satisfied in my soul and I didn't think about it anymore. However, when we met I was totally wrong about what they wanted. Sometimes merely thinking we have something figured out will comfort us, so why not just think (believe) that God has everything figured out and find comfort from that?

Concern for Our Loved Ones

Fear of the unknown certainly shows up when we begin thinking about all of the people we love who perhaps are not currently making good decisions. We wonder what may happen to them if they don't make some healthy changes in their lives. Each person ultimately has the responsibility of making their own decisions, and we cannot control their decisions through any amount of worry or concern. Thankfully, we can pray; when we do, God will deal with them and give them every opportunity to turn their lives in a good direction. If an opportunity presents itself, we may be able to speak a word of wisdom, direction, or even correction when appropriate, but we cannot control other people's destinies no matter how much we would like to.

We worry about our children when they are growing up—especially the ones who seem to have "issues." One of my daughters and one of my sons hated school and honestly didn't care what kind of grades they got. I remember worrying a lot about what would happen to them in the future because they both only wanted to have fun and seemed to have no concern at all beyond that. But if we fast-forward 25 years, the son I mentioned is now one of two CEOs of Joyce Meyer Ministries. At the age of 33, he handles a tremendous amount of responsibility and does an excellent job. You see that all of the worrying was useless. Thankfully, I did some praying, and God heard those prayers along with the prayers of others and things have turned out fine. The daughter I mentioned who could barely keep track of herself at the age of 17 now helps me keep my life organized! She is a wife and mother of four children and handles a great deal of responsibility. I believe I can say with assurance that if you pray for your loved ones, God will go to work. And one thing is certain: If God cannot convince a person to change, we certainly cannot. Today you can choose to cast the care of your loved ones onto God and let Him take care of them. Pray and trust that God is working no matter what you see or feel.

Fear of the unknown can be ever-present unless we come to terms with it. God knows what we don't know, and He loves us and will always take care of us. Beyond that, there isn't much we have to know, and whatever we do need to know, God will surely reveal at the right time.

CHAPTER 16

The Fear of Making Mistakes

Our doubts are our traitors, and make us lose the good we oft might win, by fearing to attempt.

William Shakespeare

Many people battle with a powerful fear of making a wrong choice or a poor decision—so they make no decision at all! They remain in indecision. They mentally go over and over their options, yet never find one that they can settle on. They want a guarantee of perfection before they are willing to take action, but sadly, unless we take risks we will never decide anything at all. Multitudes of people are inactive and frozen in fear simply because they are unwilling to make a mistake.

Like most fears, the fear of making mistakes has a name, and it is called "decidophobia." It is an overwhelming, irrational fear of making decisions. People with this phobia do not make decisions. Of course, not everyone has "decidophobia," but many people are double-minded and they find decision making difficult. The good news is that there is a cure for decidophobia and it is called "doing it afraid"! Feel the fear and do it anyway!

Wasted time, or even a wasted life, is somehow not as fearful to the indecisive person as making a mistake! Individuals with a "perfectionist" bent can be especially prone to this fear. At the foundation of their temperament is a driving desire to be perfect, and they often spend many agonizing years coming to grips with the reality that we all make mistakes. A mistake is an event, not a person. We may make mistakes, but *we* are not mistakes!

God invites us to an adventurous life of boldness and creativity, of exploration and variety, but we will miss it if we live in the fear of making mistakes. Do you want a narrow life with no adventure, or a broad one filled with adventure and new things?

Structure

There is certainly nothing wrong with structure, and in fact, we all need it. Structure is a good thing and there is safety in it, but when our lives must be so structured that we never veer away from sameness into newness, then we are closing the door to the best life that God wants us to have. God is a God of order and structure, but He also loves and invites us into passionate creativity. Although God is a God of order, I have found that when I follow the leadership of the Holy Spirit on a daily basis, my life is filled with twists and turns that I didn't plan or expect. They make life exciting. It is quite impossible to remain enthusiastic about eternal sameness.

Sameness is safe, but it is also very boring, and when people are bored they often get themselves into trouble. When people are bored with life they may blame their unhappiness on the people they are the closest to. It becomes the fault of the person they are married to, or their job, or their church, or whatever else they can find to blame it on. A person may feel unfulfilled in their marriage, so they get a divorce and try someone else. They quit a good job and spend their lives going from job to job and never excelling at anything. Maybe instead of a divorce, what they really need is adding some spice to the marriage they already have. Do something new! Go somewhere! Work at your marriage, and instead of passively waiting for your partner to make some changes, do something that is a bit on the edge yourself. Plan a surprise vacation, or get tickets to a play or musical. Do something you wouldn't ordinarily do and add some spice to life. A food can be boringly plain and taste bland, but if we add a little of the right spice it changes the taste and we may love it.

If you're bored with your job, why not apply for a transfer to another department or a promotion within the company where you will have more responsibility? If you're bored with yourself, then why not try a new haircut, or maybe an "out of the box" clothing style once in a while? Maybe you won't even end up liking it, but then it will help you appreciate what you have. The fear of making mistakes is the only thing that prevents people from living more aggressively. We think, *What if I take a new position at work and end up not liking it?* Or, *What if I plan a surprise for my spouse and he or she doesn't want to do it?* The "what ifs" in life can steal all of the enthusiasm from it, and they can even derail our destiny.

When we are unhappy and dissatisfied, the first place we should look is at ourselves. We can ask ourselves if our relationship with God is in good condition and whether or not we are following the leadership of the Holy Spirit. I believe the Holy Spirit always leads us to "abundant life," and if that is not what we are experiencing we should seek to know why.

Many people love God, but they remain fearful of making decisions that will lead them into new things. They might be afraid to teach the Sunday school class they have been feeling prompted by the Holy Spirit to lead. They might be afraid to make a

> *The thing that stands between where we are and where we want to be is always doing the thing we don't want to do.*

commitment to a small-group Bible study. They are not sure they want to get that involved with other people, so they remain lonely and bored. The thing that stands between where we are and where we want to be is always doing the thing we don't want to do.

God has sent His Holy Spirit to live in our hearts, to lead, guide, and direct us into all truth and the best life that we can have. But He cannot lead us anywhere if we are not willing to follow. The apostle Paul had an amazing life and ministry, and we can see in his writings that he followed the leadership of the Holy Spirit to the best of his ability. Yet there were times when he made mistakes…Yes, I said the apostle Paul made mistakes! His missionary journeys included many stops, and at one time we see that he tried to go to Bithynia, but the Spirit of Jesus did not permit him to go (see Acts 16:17).

Paul tried to go somewhere to minister that wasn't the right place for him to be, and God simply stopped him. The Bible doesn't tell us how he was stopped, but somehow he got the message that it wasn't what God wanted him to do. Paul didn't get depressed, go hide somewhere, and feel insecure because he had made a mistake, but he simply went to the next town. If you are immobile right now due to a mistake you have made, why not shake it off and get moving again?

We can learn a lot from this account of Paul's journeys and apply the principle we see here to our own life situations. I believe in having an aggressive attitude that says, "I would rather try to do something than be satisfied with doing nothing." Paul knew that the Gospel needed to be preached, and he was busy preaching it. He was more successful some places than others, but he kept moving. He did not let the fear of being wrong or making a mistake paralyze him and prevent from doing anything at all.

This is an attitude we can adopt in our lives. We can say: "This may not be the best day I've ever had...but I'm going to keep moving." "I'm not sure if this is going to work or not...but I'm going to keep moving." "I know that the Lord has promised never to leave me...so I'm going to keep moving!"

The People We Admire

Most of us know someone in life whom we admire. We are in awe of their accomplishments and we wish it could have been us who did what they did. The thing we may not realize is that they took risks to get where they are. I recently heard someone say, "If you're not failing occasionally, then you're not taking risks." This is so true! It is virtually impossible to do great things without taking risks. We should do what we do based on biblical principles of wisdom, but it is not biblical to do absolutely nothing. Wayne Gretzky said it this way: "You'll always miss 100 percent of the shots you never take."

The parable of the talents shared in God's Word teaches us this same lesson. Three men were given three different amounts of talents (money) from their master, each according to his ability. The master told them to take care of the talents while he was on a long journey. When he returned he asked the servants for an accounting of the talents. The one who had received five talents had invested his and gained five more, and now had 10. The one who had received two talents had invested his also and gained two more. But the servant who had received one talent was afraid, and he buried his in the ground and returned to his master only the one he had been given. His master called that man wicked, lazy, and idle, and the master took his talent away from him and gave it to another (see Matthew 25:14–28). Wow! Was he a harsh master? After all, the poor man was afraid! I have come to realize that when we are afraid we can easily expect people to make special concessions for our fear, but the master didn't do that with his servants, and I don't think God does it for His servants either. He expects us to trust Him and live boldly! Even when we feel fear, He expects us to do it afraid.

We may admire the courage of the apostle Peter, who preached in the streets of Jerusalem on the day of Pentecost and added 3,000 people to the church. But let us remember that Peter showed fear prior to that. He denied Christ at the time of Jesus' crucifixion because of fear. Thomas was filled with doubt, which is merely another expression of fear. The disciples were concerned because they had failed to bring lunch even though they had seen Jesus feed thousands with a little boy's lunch. But after the death and resurrection of Jesus and the outpouring of the Holy Spirit on Pentecost, we see changed men! They were now filled with the Holy Spirit and His presence within filled them with courage like they had not known prior to that.

Every believer has the privilege of being filled with, guided, taught, and counseled by the Holy Spirit. He will lead us, and even if we miss His leading initially, He will help us get redirected. If we get off on the wrong track, God will steer us back to safety.

> *Your own ears will hear him. Right behind you a voice will say, "This is the way you should go," whether to the right or to the left.*
>
> Isaiah 30:21 (NLT)

We need not be frozen in the fear of making mistakes. God has provided a win-win plan for His people. Trust God and live boldly, and when you do make mistakes, trust God to get you back on track and use your mistake to your advantage.

Seeing what others have done, and how they have overcome mistakes, should let us know that we are capable of doing something amazing too without living in fear. I believe we are created for greatness. Everyone who has received Jesus into their lives has a seed of greatness in them. They have a desire to stretch, reach, climb, soar, and go beyond the "normal range" of living. Whatever we do, we should excel at it. We should desire to be the best we can be and do the most we can do to make the world a better place.

> *Everyone who has received Jesus into their lives has a seed of greatness in them. They have a desire to stretch, reach, climb, soar, and go beyond the "normal range" of living.*

Indecision

Being indecisive can be a huge problem if we don't conquer it. It can be caused from the fear of making mistakes, but it can also be caused due to the monumental number of choices we have facing us.

A friend who is a missionary in Africa told me a story about him and his wife that makes a good point. They seldom come to America now, but the last time they did, they wanted to get some cereal because there is only one cereal available where they live. My friend pulled up in front of the store and his wife went in but returned after over 30 minutes empty-handed. When he asked where the cereal was, she replied, "There were so many choices that I got confused and didn't get anything."

In America we like options, but we have become so excessive that it has gotten confusing. We have so many clothes that we stand in our closet for long periods feeling that we have nothing to wear. We go to restaurants with a massive menu and cannot decide what to eat. We have literally hundreds of channels on our televisions and we can spend hours flipping from one to another and never settling on any one program. Our large variety of choices has become a hindrance instead of a help to us, and at the root of it is greed! We want more and more, and in the pursuit of it all, we have become more and more confused, and often less and less satisfied.

I think we may have to aggressively practice just making a decision instead of wasting too much time trying to make one and possibly never doing so. We can focus on a few choices and then decide. You might think, *What if I missed the best one?* But you could have spent another hour trying to decide and still ended up with the choice you made. By the way, that hour is one that you will never get back. Once we use our time, whether wisely or unwisely, it is gone forever. I think it is best not to waste it!

In a California gourmet market, Professor Lyengar and her research assistants set up a booth of samples of Wilkin and Sons jams. Every few hours they switched from offering a selection of 24 jams to a group of six jams. On average, customers tasted two jams, regardless of the size of the assortment, and each one received a coupon good for $1 off one Wilkin and Sons jam.

Here is the interesting part. Sixty percent of customers were drawn to the large assortment, while only 40 percent stopped by the small one. But 30 percent of the people who had sampled from the small assortment decided to buy jam, while only 3 percent of those confronted with the two dozen jams purchased a jar. The presence of many choices may be appealing, but it seems to also be debilitating.[1]

Analysis Paralysis

The term "analysis paralysis" refers to overanalyzing or overthinking a situation. This complicates the decision-making process. When we seek the one decision that will assure us that perfection will be reached, we can rarely make any decision at all. I happen to be quite aggressive when it comes to making decisions, and if anything, I might make a few of them too quickly, but at least I make them.

I feel sorry for people who labor over every decision. Sometimes I feel that I can see them suffering. Quite often they know that other people are waiting for them to decide and that adds more pressure to the pressure they are already under. It takes courage for them to finally say, "I want this," and even when they do, they are usually still not sure they have made the right choice.

I often say that we can think a thing to death. What I mean is that we can suck all the enjoyment out of a thing by overanalyzing it. What could have been a joy turns into an irritation because we are playing mental hockey with it, knocking it all over the place and never making a goal. If you tend to be indecisive and excessively analytical, why not declare war on indecision and bravely go forward with a brand-new decisive attitude? Perhaps a new attitude toward mistakes would help!

A New Attitude Toward Mistakes

Focus on these things:

- Everyone makes mistakes and it is no big deal.
- There are very few mistakes that we cannot recover from. Take longer with the really big decisions, but don't stress over all the small stuff.
- Just because you may make a mistake doesn't mean YOU are a mistake.
- God sent Jesus for people who make mistakes.
- You don't have to be perfect to be accepted.
- If you don't take risks, you will live a boring life.
- You cannot make progress without making decisions.
- Most of the mistakes you make bother YOU more than they bother anyone else.
- All of your mistakes are merely a lesson in progress.
- Think more about the many things you do right than the few things you do wrong.

Having a healthy attitude toward things is vital if we want to enjoy life. Whether it is regarding mistakes, failures, problems, or losses, the right attitude can change everything. It can turn tragedy into triumph, pain into gain, and mistakes into miracles. You own your attitude and it is the one thing that nobody can take away from you. You and you alone can decide what kind of an attitude you will have in every situation in life, and the attitude you choose determines your level of enjoyment of life. Decide today to live boldly and no longer be afraid of making mistakes.

CHAPTER 17

The Fear of God's Anger and Judgment

*The Lord is gracious and full of compassion, slow to anger
and abounding in mercy and loving-kindness.*

Psalm 145:8

It grieves me to see people live with a fear that God is angry with them because of their sins, weaknesses, and mistakes. God does hate sin, but He loves sinners and is ever-ready to forgive and restore us when we do sin. Don't receive the lie from Satan that when you have trials and difficulties in your life God is punishing you for your sins. Although disobedience can bring unpleasant results, we must remember that when we ask God to forgive our sins He removes them as far as the east is from the west—He remembers them no more (see Psalm 103:10–12). Our sins don't have to separate us from God's goodness unless we let them. If God only blessed perfect people, then nobody would ever receive blessings in their lives.

The inherent nature of God is that He is good! He is good all the time, and He only does what works for good in our lives. We live in a world that is not always good, and at times bad things happen to good people. When they do, it is not fair, but God never told us that life would always be fair. He does promise us that He is a God of justice, which means He will ultimately, in His own proper timing, make all wrong things right. That promise gives me great comfort and it fuels my faith to continue believing God for good things even in the midst of trouble.

I am particularly fond of the following verse of Scripture...

> *Every good gift and every perfect (free, large, full) gift is from above; it comes down from the Father of all [that gives] light, in [the shining of] Whom there can be no variation [rising or setting] or shadow cast by His turning [as in an eclipse].*
>
> James 1:17

Everything good comes from God. We don't earn or deserve God's goodness, but thankfully we are on the receiving end of it. He is good because it is His nature to be good, and the Scripture above tells us that there is not even the slightest turning or variation in God's goodness. It is impossible to live without the fear of God's anger and judgment if we don't fully believe that God is good to the very core of His being. Let me say again, GOD IS GOOD and He delights in being good to you! If we don't believe He is good, then we will automatically believe that He is angry with us every time we make a mistake. We will also expect judgment and punishment from Him.

My father was an angry man, and anytime I did not please him I got punishment of some kind, but God is *not* like that. The truth is that we can repent of our sins, and instead of expecting anger and punishment, we can expect the enjoyment of God's presence and blessing. God is not looking for an excuse to punish us; He looks, longs, and waits to be good to us.

> *And therefore the Lord [earnestly] waits [expecting, looking, and longing] to be gracious to you; and therefore He lifts*

Himself up, that He may have mercy on you and show loving-kindness to you.

Isaiah 30:18

This verse says plainly that God wants to be good to us. It goes on to say that He is looking for someone who is waiting for Him to be good to them. What are you expecting in your life? Do you focus on your mistakes and expect God to punish you for them, or do you repent of them and expect God to forgive you and show you His favor, blessing, and goodness?

I believe we should look for the goodness of God in our lives and make a really big deal out of it. Sadly, we often make a big deal out of our problems and challenges and barely notice God's goodness. What we focus on is what looms the largest in our lives; therefore, we should fix our focus on things that increase our joy, not on things that steal it. If we don't take notice of the good things that God does in our lives, we are in danger of beginning to think that somehow we

> What we focus on is what looms the largest in our lives; therefore, we should fix our focus on things that increase our joy, not on things that steal it.

have missed them and that perhaps God doesn't love us as much as the people who have it good in life. Just imagine: We could be extremely blessed and not even be aware of it just because we focus on the negative things we experience instead of the good ones.

Janet is a woman in her early fifties and she is the wife of Harry and mother to Andrew, Joshua, and Lacy. They have a nice home, are financially secure, and are all in good health. Over the past five years Janet has grown increasingly depressed, and when she is asked what is wrong, she readily offers a long list of complaints.

Her house is too small, her husband works too much, she never has any fun in life, too much is expected of her, and it seems that nothing good ever happens to her. A woman we will call Ann has recently met Janet through another acquaintance, and she has no family, has diabetes, and suffers from fairly serious back pain on most days. She also lost her job of 20 years recently, has had to start over in an entirely different line of work, and the pay is much less than what she is accustomed to.

As Ann listened to Janet lament her problems, she told Janet that she would trade lives with her in a second. She said, "You have someone who comes home at night that you can do things for and talk to. You have children who love you and that you can be proud of, you have good health and that is one of the greatest gifts you can have." Ann went on describing the blessings she recognized in Janet's life. Ann saw Janet's blessings, but Janet could not see them because her perspective was damaged. She looked at her life and saw blessings she didn't have that others did have, instead of looking at problems she didn't have that she could have had if God had not been protecting her from them.

Sometimes after driving home in heavy traffic I think, *I wonder how many accidents I would have had today if God wasn't protecting me?* When I get unhappy because I weigh three pounds more than my "target weight," I try to remember the woman I met who had a metabolism disorder and was 150 pounds overweight. I spent a lot of years unhappy, like Janet, until I finally decided to be happy on purpose, and one of the ways I accomplish that is by counting my blessings—magnifying them, making a big deal out of them, celebrating them, and being thankful for all of them.

Some of you might be thinking, *Joyce, I don't really see that many blessings in my life, nor do I feel that God is good to me. I have had lots of loss and trouble in my life.* If that is you, I want to strongly encourage you to "fix your focus," and begin to seriously consider all of the ways that God is helping, protecting, and providing for you. Are you breathing today? If so, then you are a recipient of God's goodness. Do you have a home, a job, family, or friends? If the answer is yes, then you are experiencing the goodness of God. Do you have food to eat, clean water to drink, clothes to wear, and can you walk, talk, hear, and see? If so, you should be rejoicing that God is good to you. Perhaps you don't have all of these things, but you do have some of them and you can rejoice in what you do have. I can assure you that no matter how difficult your circumstances are right now, there are countless people in much worse conditions than you.

Don't Blame God

I recently met a woman while shopping who shared with me that she had experienced tremendous loss in her life, and because of it, she felt that she could no longer trust God. This is the case with many people. They are angry at God because things have not worked out the way they thought they should have in their lives. I am always saddened to see someone with this mind-set because God is their friend, not the cause of their troubles. They blame God for their troubles when they should trust Him to help them get through the troubles.

Just as I know people who blame God for their problems, I also know people who have experienced great tragedy and their testimony is still, "God is good!" We cannot determine the goodness of God by the amount of loss and pain we have in our lives. Trouble comes for many different reasons, but God is not the source of our disappointments and troubles. Some even erroneously believe that when they experience hardship in life that God is punishing them for their sins, but they are wrong. Our troubles don't come from God. We do, however, have an enemy named Satan, or the devil, and he does relentlessly come against us. His goal is to kill, steal, and destroy, but Jesus came to give us life and that more abundantly (see John 10:10).

I cannot totally explain why some people have more difficulty in life than others do, but I do know that God never allows more to come on us than we can bear, and He always provides a way out if we trust Him (see 1 Corinthians 10:13). His deliverance may not come in the amount of time we would prefer, but it will come at the right time. If we do not get delivered from our difficulty, then God will give us the grace to endure with a good attitude.

> God never allows more to come on us than we can bear, and He always provides a way out if we trust Him.

Our goal should be to remain stable and strong in faith and never to think God no longer loves us because we are having problems.

How can we even reasonably say that we have had more trouble than other people? After all, we don't know all that goes on in other people's lives. We are not to compare ourselves with other people anyway, but if we were to try, we would have to compare an entire life with an entire life, not one event compared to another. What I mean is we may be having difficulty, so when we look at someone else who seems to be in the midst of many good things that are taking place in their lives we make a comparison, but we don't know what they have gone through in the past, or for that matter, what they may still have to go through in their future. I tend to think that we all have our share of difficulty before our lives are over. God's Word tells us that suffering is appointed to the whole body of Christians throughout the world (see 1 Peter 5:9). We must remember that if we never had any trials we would have no need for any faith in God. Faith trusts God for good things that we don't see yet, but that we believe are forthcoming. Until we have them manifested in our lives, we have them by faith! We have the privilege of believing that God's promises are true!

We are urged to withstand the devil (who is the author of all bad things)—to be vigilant against him at all times, for he roams around like a lion roaring in fierce hunger, seeking someone whom he may devour (see 1 Peter 5:8–9). We don't have to trust in our own strength to withstand the devil—we have the privilege of trusting God! We can enter the rest of God and enjoy our lives while God deals with our enemies and problems.

I spoke this morning with a man whose sister-in-law died at the age of 40 with cancer. She left behind young children and a husband, siblings, and parents, all of whom are very sad and deeply feeling their loss. But none of them are blaming God! I also know of a wonderful pastor who recently lost his beautiful wife due to cancer, and I am happy to say that I have not once heard him blame God for his pain and loss. As a matter of fact, he told me personally that he would never ask God "why" she died so young. He felt that out of respect for God, he should continue trusting God as he had done in the past, and keep working even more diligently in his ministry to others. I was so proud of him and very inspired by his attitude of faith in the midst of adversity.

How can some people have such a good attitude during times of loss and pain, while others are quick to blame God and even feel that they did something wrong in their lives and they are being punished? It has a lot to do with how well we really know our God, and our willingness to trust Him even when it makes no sense to our natural mind. Sometimes we can see the reasons why things happen, but most of the time they are none of our business,

Trust doesn't have to know why.

and we should not even need a reason for everything anyway. Trust doesn't have to know why.

You might think that is not good enough for you, and that you must know why bad things happen to good people, while bad people seem to be blessed. I don't think I have an all-inclusive answer, but I do know a few things that I will share. First, the devil is the author of all evil things, and he is still roaming the earth spreading his misery. There are times when our faith is tested and we feel as if we are sheep being led to the slaughter (see Romans 8:36), but we are promised that even then we are more than conquerors through Christ who loves us (see Romans 8:37).

Choose to Believe

When I talked with the woman I met while shopping that I mentioned before, I told her she had two options. One was to continue on as she was, and she had said herself that she was lonely and miserable due to shutting God out of her life. Or, I suggested—actually I pleaded with her—that she could choose to trust God even in the midst of the loss she was experiencing. I know that God wants to help this woman, but she needs to open the door through believing He is good and asking Him to do the best thing for her.

One thing that God does require of us is that we believe in Him and His promises to us. He does all the work of providing, but we cannot receive unless we believe. Believing is free, it doesn't cost us anything, so why not do it? It is a decision we can make, and one that opens doors of possibility. Believing releases joy and peace (see Romans 15:13), and anything other than that drags us down mentally, emotionally, spiritually, and even physically. We need hope in order to live happy lives, and our only true hope is found in God.

We overcome fear with faith! No matter what kind of fear it is, even the fear of God's anger and judgment can be defeated through simple faith and believing as a child would.

God Is Not Mad at You

While I was growing up as a child I always feared that I would get into trouble because my father was an angry man, and it was a great relief to me when I discovered that Father God is not like that at all. I suffered greatly with the pangs of guilt and fear of being punished each time I did even the slightest thing wrong. I felt when things were not going well in my life that I was receiving punishment from God, and that I needed to do better. My believing was wrong! I didn't know God, nor did I know His character. I thought He was like my earthly father, but that was not true at all.

God can get angry, but He is not an "angry God." He is good, full of mercy and compassion, quick to forgive and slow to anger. God's anger is toward sin, not sinners. The Bible teaches us that Jesus is a friend of sinners. His goodness draws men to repentance. He hates sin because He knows that it produces death in our lives. It steals every good thing that God has in mind for us. God works to draw us into a love relationship with Him, away from sin and misery, and He doesn't do it by heaping tragedy and loss on us as payment for our past mistakes.

Millions of people suffer because of the deception that God is mad at them, just as I did, so last year I wrote an entire book on the topic and I recommend it for your further education on this subject. It is simply titled *Perfect Love*.

Don't Let the Devil Blackmail You

A story is told of a little boy who accidentally killed his grand-mother's pet duck. He hit the duck with a rock from his sling-shot while he was playing. The boy didn't think that anyone saw the foul deed, so he buried the duck in the backyard and didn't tell a soul.

Later the boy found out that his sister had seen the entire thing. Not only that, she now had the leverage of his secret and used it. Whenever it was the sister's turn to wash the dishes, take out the garbage, or wash the car, she would whis-per in his ear, "Remember the duck." And then the little boy would do what his sister should have done.

There is always a limit to that sort of thing. Finally, he couldn't take it anymore—he'd had it! The boy went to his grandmother and, with great fear, confessed what he had done. To his surprise, she hugged him and thanked him. She said, "I was standing at the kitchen sink and saw the whole thing. I forgave you then. I was just wondering when you were going to get tired of your sister's blackmail and come to me."

> Jesus took all the punishment and judgment we deserve from God, and we are free to come to Him and enter into an intimate relationship of love and acceptance.

Jesus took all the punishment and judgment we deserve from God, and we are free to come to Him and enter into an intimate relationship of love and acceptance. Just as the lit-tle boy's grandmother was probably waiting to give him a big hug, God is waiting to give us one, if we will just stop letting the devil blackmail us.

God is focused on you and His love for you, not on what you have done wrong in your life. Instead of you focusing on what you have done wrong and the punishment you are afraid of getting, focus on God's love and mercy. Run to Father God and get your hug! Focus on the fact that He is good at all times, and continue believing in His promises no matter what your circumstances look like. Things are always changing, but God never changes. He loves us forever and will never leave us nor forsake us.

CHAPTER 18

The Fear of Intimacy

For the Law never made anything perfect—but instead a better hope is introduced through which we [now] come close to God.

Hebrews 7:19

Intimacy is extreme closeness. Through Jesus we are offered a close, intimate relationship with God. Many are afraid of intimacy with people and also with God. But the truth is that you can be as close to God as you want to be. He is waiting for you, and there are no limitations on the wonderful relationship you can have with Him if you truly desire it. You can also have close, intimate relationships with people; but in saying that, I must also tell you that vulnerability is required, and you cannot have one without the other.

We often forfeit intimacy because we don't want to take a chance on being hurt. We are afraid that if people really get to know us intimately, they may not like us, or be shocked by the truth they see. I heard that "intimacy" means "Into-Me-See." That says it all. If we want intimacy, we must be willing to let people see into us and we must be willing to see into them and not be shocked or appalled by what we find. But before we get too far into discussing intimacy with people, let's discuss intimacy with God.

Intimacy with God

Under the Old Covenant legalistic system that demanded the following of rules and regulations, people did not frequently experience intimacy or closeness with God. They merely tried to please Him by keeping rules and they made sacrifices of animals and other things to pay for their mistakes. This system kept them busy, but it didn't bring them close to God. A wall of separation was forever erected between God and man. God is holy and men are sinners, and their sin separates them from God. Thankfully, God was not willing to leave us in that condition. He had a plan for our deliverance, and His Name is Jesus Christ, the Son of God, who took on the form of a human being and came to Earth to pay for our sins and open wide the door of access to God.

On the day that Jesus died and paid for the sins of man, the skies became dark and the earth shook and the thick veil or curtain in the Temple that separated the holy place from the Most Holy Place was torn in half from top to bottom (see Luke 23:44–45). Ordinary people had never been allowed to go beyond the separating curtain into the Most Holy Place where God's presence dwelt; only the high priest could enter once a year (see Hebrews 9:6–7). So this tearing of the veil was very meaningful to them. It was God saying loud and clear, *"Come close to Me...you're welcome in My presence."*

Previously, even the thought of being in God's presence terrified the people, so this was a big change for them. God was willing to be intimate with them, but were they willing to be intimate with Him? Are we willing to be intimate with God? Are we willing to let Him into every area of our lives? These are big questions and they should not be answered without some serious forethought.

Are there areas in your life that you are unwilling to open to God? What if you invited Him in and He asked you to change something that you don't want to change? Or what if He asks you to do something that you don't want to do? Those thoughts frighten us, so we protect our private spaces, and in the process we forfeit intimacy with God. It is interesting to note that God already knows everything about us, but He won't force His way into any area of our lives. He waits to be invited. God wants to be wanted!

Would you be willing to pray this prayer right now?

Father God, I invite You into every area of my life. I want You to have full access to everything concerning me. I want You to take the lead and teach me how to follow You. I surrender all to You and I trust that Your ways are better than mine. You are welcome to direct my thoughts, my words, my attitudes, all of my actions, my entertainment, my finances, and my plans for the future. Teach me Your ways. I desire intimacy with You. I want close fellowship with You. Thank You for a new beginning, in Jesus' name!

If you prayed that prayer, you might want to buckle your seat belt for the ride of your life. God's ways are not our ways, but His ways are much better. They may shock you at first, and God will probably show you some things that you don't necessarily want to look at, but the value of intimacy with God is inestimable, immeasurable, and greater than anything you can imagine.

Intimacy with People

For me, intimacy with God has been much easier to develop than intimacy with people. People are not perfect, they can be disappointing, and their expectations are quite unreasonable at times. Without sounding negative, which I do not want to do, I feel I need to say that developing intimacy with people is challenging. First of all, it takes peo-

> *Getting to know people intimately takes time, understanding, and a willingness to be deeply honest.*

ple who are willing to work through the process in order to have intimacy. Getting to know people intimately takes time, understanding, and a willingness to be deeply honest. Although there may be some things that are reserved for only God and us, we will need to open up and let people into our private space to some degree. The level of intimacy we enjoy will partially depend on how open we are willing to be.

Our Secrets

Some people's secrets are making them sick. They have things hidden inside of them that eat away at them. They live in fear of people finding out what their secret is, but the best thing they could possibly do is find someone they can trust and start talking, confessing, venting, and in short, unloading the things that frighten and imprison them. Once a thing is exposed it loses its power over you. It is only the things hidden in darkness that Satan uses to threaten us.

April had an abortion when she was 17 years old. Her boyfriend, who was older than she, made all the arrangements, and April never told anyone. She felt guilty and was fearful that God would punish her for what she had done. April lived her life with this secret burden. She met a man when she was 22; they fell in love and got married, but the relationship was strained. She still had her secret burden!

A few years went by and they wanted to have children, but April never got pregnant. She was convinced that God was punishing her for the abortion, but still she had not shared her secret with her husband. The doctor assured her there was no medical reason why she and her husband could not have children, and he suggested that her inability to conceive was due to stress. In the midst of this dilemma, April reached out to God and received Jesus as her Savior. She felt so much better after unloading her burden to God that she decided to share with her husband. She was fearful of his judgment once he knew her secret, but just the opposite occurred. He was of course surprised, but he understood that she was young and had made a mistake. He forgave her for not being open with him, and finally April was able to relax in God's love and her husband's. Within three months April was pregnant and they now have three children and a wonderful life.

I kept the secret of the sexual abuse I experienced for many long years, and when I finally did share it, my burden began to get lighter. I needed years of healing, but the beginning of all healing is dealing with your pain openly and honestly.

There are some secrets that we don't need to share. I strongly believe there are some things that should always remain between God and us. Some of those things might be secret things that we believe He has said to us, or shown us. They might not be understood by others, and people's reactions might discourage and disappoint us.

I also believe we should not tell people things that will devastate them while doing them no good. We should not relieve our burden at the cost of giving one to someone else. For example, I once had a lady come to me after hearing me teach on being truthful, and she wanted to share with me how she had always disliked me and now wanted to ask me to forgive her. Of course, I did tell her she was forgiven, but her confession put all kinds of questions in my mind about what I may have done to make her dislike me. She got rid of her problem, but she gave me one. This is not healthy intimacy, and if we are going to seek intimacy we must realize that it needs to be healthy for both parties.

Confrontation

Intimacy may require some godly confrontation. You may desire an improved relationship with someone who has hurt you, or continues to hurt you with words or actions, and a deeper relationship with them is not possible as long as you feel you need to have your guard up each time you are with them. Pray first, choose a right time, and share with them in a loving way. Confrontation almost always makes a relationship better or worse. If it makes it better, then you can move on to deeper levels of friendship; if it makes it worse, then you may lose a friend. The search for deeper and more meaningful relationships can be costly.

I don't give up on relationships easily. I have had to confront and be confronted in several situations and have found that if we both continue to work through the issues at hand, our relationship gets stronger. However, let me say again, it does take two people who are willing. You are only responsible for your part, so do your best and trust God to give good healthy relationships.

Symptoms and Roots of the Fear of Intimacy

People who fear intimacy are not willing to share emotions and true feelings. They pretend that they are fine when they aren't, and appear to be untouched by anything when the reality is that inside they are wounded and bleeding.

They are very private in an unbalanced way. We do of course have a right to privacy, but intimacy is not possible unless we are willing to let the one we desire to have intimacy with into some areas of our private life. I happen to be a very open person, and since I am, I tend to ask a lot of questions that could appear to be none of my business. I often tell people, "If I am getting into things you are not comfortable with, just tell me." Sharing my past and even my current faults openly is one of the things God has used to set me free, and I believe it is one of the things He uses to help others through my teaching. I am gifted with openness, but not everyone is and we should always respect people's privacy. However, if individuals are unwilling to let people into any area of their lives, then intimacy and closeness are not possible.

While I am writing this section, I am also attending a manager's retreat for our leadership team. I talked with them about the importance of facing and admitting our weaknesses. I asked a few people what they thought their greatest weakness was and as they openly shared, it ended up helping several other people. One of the managers later said, "We have been talking among ourselves and we think that if we shared our weaknesses more openly instead of living in fear of people finding out about them, we could really help each other, and our bond would become stronger." I said, "Amen!"

Those who fear intimacy generally feel threatened when they think someone is going to ask them about private matters. They have many fears concerning themselves, and they've practiced hiding for so long that the fear of people truly knowing them is overwhelmingly frightening. People with this fear may have many surface relationships, but they quickly escape any relationship that starts to go deeper.

Past hurts, or trauma of some kind, are almost always the root of the fear of intimacy. God has created us with a desire for connectedness, and when we fear it, there is always a reason. People want to be connected with others, but they are often afraid of the process, so they live isolated and lonely lives. We should do it afraid and begin to enjoy the beauty of genuine, close relationships. I have found that the Bible is a book about relationships. It is about our relationship with God, our relationship with our self, and our relationships with other people. All of these should be healthy and emotionally satisfying.

There are many reasons for the fear of intimacy, but thankfully we can overcome those fears and enjoy close, healthy, and intimate relationships. Getting to the root of our problems is step one toward freedom, and step two is being unwilling to remain that way once we figure out the root problem. Thankfully, we can fully understand why we are a certain way and still not be willing to remain that way. Jesus died to restore to us all that was lost to us through sin and evil, and we should pursue it with the help of the Holy Spirit. My connection with my parents was dysfunctional to say the least. I certainly did not learn from them how to have healthy, intimate relationships, but I have learned it from the Word of God and the leadership of the Holy Spirit. The Holy Spirit is our Teacher, and if we are willing to lay aside our fears, He will lead us into satisfying and close relationships.

Ways to Develop Better Relationships

One of the reasons why people have difficulty connecting closely with others is a lack of social interest. They may be workaholics

If we want people to be interested in us, then we must learn to be interesting.

who have found their worth and value in work alone. They have very few, if any, interests, and therefore have no basis for connection. If we want people to be interested in us, then we must learn to be interesting. One thing we can do is educate ourselves in things that others are interested in so we have a broader basis for conversation. Dave loves sports and watches almost all of the various games that are on television. Quite often in the morning I will ask him who won the baseball game, or the football game, or the golf match. I ask, not because I am that interested in the sport, but I am interested in him. I know that he enjoys talking about sports, and one way I can connect with him is to listen. When he goes to play golf, I always ask him about his game that day. If we are interested in what others are interested in, then it makes us interesting to them. It provides a connection between us and is a good starting point for more meaningful relationships.

Another way to connect with people is to know what they like and enjoy so you can help provide it for them. If we do nothing for one another, then we have no part in each other's lives. If we truly listen to people, they tell us what they like, want, or need, and it becomes easy to make them happy. When we make people happy or help them to feel good about themselves, they always like us. People may not remember everything you say to them, but they always remember how you made them feel.

There are many ways to develop better relationships. Listening is one of the ways. Being honest at all times and keeping our word and commitments are two others. Intimate relationships are built on trust. Clear communication is also vital. Go the extra mile to communicate, and if you cannot keep a commitment, explain why you cannot instead of merely ignoring it. Always be quick to say, "I'm sorry," if and when you hurt or disappoint someone. Keep people's secrets. When a spouse, relative, or friend does share an intimate detail of their life with you, be sure that you keep the information private between you and them. If they want someone else to know, it is their place to share it and not yours. Generally speaking, if we treat others the way we want to be treated, we are well on our way to developing great relationships.

Real Intimacy

Real intimacy is a lot more than sex. Sex may represent physical intimacy, but if that is all there is, then it is shallow to say the least. True intimacy between a husband and wife must be shared on all levels, not merely in the bedroom. Couples need to talk openly and be equally understood by each other. It always creates difficulty in marriages when one person deeply desires this and the other one either doesn't want it or doesn't know how to develop it.

Personality comes into play when we are trying to develop intimacy. I am naturally more of a talker than my husband is, so I share more readily than he does. I always want him to talk those things out that I am going through and have him "understand," and he prefers to get through his difficulties privately and then perhaps tell me after they are over. We would all like for everyone to be like we are, but they are not and we must accept that. True closeness can only be experienced when we respect one another's differences.

> *True closeness can only be experienced when we respect one another's differences.*

If I am going through something and Dave can tell I am not acting as I normally would, he is fine if I want to share and fine if I don't. He respects my private space and I respect his. Intimacy does not mean that we pry into every area of someone else's life.

No Fear

It is not God's will that we live in any kind of fear. Remember, God does not give us a spirit of fear (see 2 Timothy 1:7). I urge you to trust God's Word and know beyond a shadow of a doubt that He deeply desires an intimate relationship with you and wants you to enjoy intimate relationships with others. God cares about everything that ever has concerned, does concern, or will concern you. He wants to be involved in every area of your life. God's will is for us to have healthy, nurturing, and satisfying relationships with other people. We should work with God to develop these relationships with family and friends. Some people by natural temperament need more people in their lives than others do, but we all need *someone*. No person is intended to live disconnected from others. I cannot promise you that you will never get hurt in relationships; as a matter of fact, I can promise you that you probably will, but the reward is worth the risk in the end. As we go through things together in relationships it brings us closer to one another, so don't give up and live an isolated, lonely life filled with the fear of intimacy.

God knows everything there is to know about each of us, and He loves us anyway. I want relationships with people like that, and I am sure you do too. I believe there are what I call "divine connections" for us all. They are relationships that God provides that will be deeply satisfying for us. Continue trusting God to lead you in developing intimate, healthy relationships; it is not His will that you live an isolated and lonely life due to fear.

CHAPTER 19

Are You Passing Your Fears on to Your Children?

He who fears the Lord has a secure fortress, and for his children it will be a refuge.

Proverbs 14:26 (NIV)

According to many verses in Scripture, a reverential fear of God can be passed on to our children—and that is a good thing. They can learn from us the value of having a right relationship with God through faith. The life we live in front of our children has a dynamic effect on them; therefore, we surely want to be careful what we are passing on to them. If we can influence them with our faith and reverential fear, awe, and respect for God, I have to believe that we can also influence them with fears that are instigated by the devil.

A famous child psychiatrist by the name of Fritz Redl was known to instruct groups of parents by saying, "Get out your paper and pencils. I am going to tell you the three most important things you will ever need to know about raising children." With pencils in hand, the parents would wait breathlessly, ready for the words of wisdom from this renowned instructor. Then he would say, "Example, example, example."[1]

The example that a parent sets is perhaps the most powerful

tool in raising children. And we need to keep that in mind when dealing with fear. Let's say a mother is fearful of being in large crowds, and for that reason, she hardly ever goes into a crowded place with her children. She even voices her fear of crowds repeatedly, and of course her children hear her quite often. There is a good possibility that her children will grow up being afraid of venturing into the new experience of being in a crowded place. Had they started early in life being in crowded places, they could have adjusted well to these conditions, but with the influence of their mother's fears, it may be difficult for them to adjust to the stress of the experience.

It is wise to let our children experience all kinds of different things. If they are introduced to them wisely, in a timely manner, then they will adapt to them and feel quite comfortable.

I am getting a new Maltese puppy soon. The breed is very small, and in my reading I learned that if the puppy is properly introduced to larger dogs, it will play well with them and have no fear. However, a friend of mine just took her one-year-old Maltese to a two-week boot camp for dogs needing to be trained in obedience. They learned within the first two days that, according to the trainer, she was "socially rude" and needed a special collar for her training. The puppy didn't know how to react to other animals simply because she had never been around them. She barked constantly as a method of self-protection.

I am sure that in our own human way we also "bark" when we are afraid of things. We go into self-protection overdrive, and our children see our responses and assume they should respond the same way we do to situations.

A woman noticed her daughter watching television and biting her nails. When she asked the child why she was biting her nails, she said, "Because you do, Mom." How much do our children learn from us, without us saying a word? Probably more than we want to recognize. Our example to those around us, especially to our children, is actually quite amazing. We can begin to take on the traits of others and not even be aware that we are doing it. This is a benefit if those traits and behaviors are good, but it is not if they are bad.

I believe what our children see us do consistently has a greater impact on them than our words do. Take for example a mom or dad who tells their children not to lie, but then they lie on a regular basis. If I tell my child to answer the phone and tell the caller I am not at home, when I clearly am at home, then I am teaching my child that dishonesty is acceptable behavior. I could even punish my child when they lie, but my example will be the thing that sticks in their mind the most. When we tell our children one thing and they see us doing the opposite of what we have instructed them to do, it is quite confusing to them and causes them not to respect us.

Do You Want Your Children to Be Brave?

If we want our children to be brave and unhindered by fear, then we must be committed to setting—and maintaining—a proper example for them. The apostle Paul encouraged Timothy to "be an example (pattern) for the believers in speech, in conduct, in love, in faith, and in purity" (1 Timothy 4:12). Our lives should be a "pattern" for other believers, but we must start by being a pattern for our own children. We should teach them not to do things that are too dangerous or age-inappropriate for them, yet at the same time teach them to live courageously. This can be done through words and setting an example.

One of our grandsons seemed to be fearful of quite a few

things: water, flying, trying new things, and my dog, just to name a few. My son did a great job of helping him face those fears and get over them. He taught him about fear and bravery, and anytime the boy did seem afraid, he told him to say, "I am not afraid; I am brave." He would also do the thing the boy was afraid of and say, "See? Daddy is doing it and nothing bad is happening." This process had to be repeated hundreds of times, if not more, but it did work. My grandson now asks to come and see my dog, goes swimming any chance he gets, is no longer afraid of airplanes, and is getting ready to be on a soccer team—a totally *new* thing for him.

Had my son only told him not to be afraid, I doubt that it would have done much good. But his patient persistence and good example was successful. If you want your children to be brave, you will need to make a commitment to teach them by word and example. I don't recommend forcing your children to do things they are afraid of, but you can lovingly work with them, and of course pray for them. Then you will see fear bow its knee to bravery.

> If you want your children to be brave, you will need to make a commitment to teach them by word and example.

If you happen to have a lot of fears yourself, you may think that it is impossible to teach your children to be brave, but the truth is that your love for them and desire to see them live free from fear may help you confront your own fears.

One mother said that she suffered so much from fear and anxiety in her life, she could not stand the thought of passing it on to her two daughters. She determined that she would do things that she was afraid of in order to be a good example to them. Love is a stronger motivator than fear! God's perfect love casts fear out of us (see 1 John 4:18), and our love for our children can prevent us from passing our fears on to them.

Your love for your children can force you out of your comfort zone. It can lead you to drive on the highway even though you might have to squeeze the steering wheel so hard your knuckles turn white. Try new things, and explain to your children that you're going to try even if you fail. By doing this you can help them not fear failure themselves. You can try new food even if you would rather not, get in the swimming pool even if you spend all your time in the shallow end, and do many other things that you ordinarily would not do. You can nurture bravery in your children's lives!

Avoid Breeding Fear in Your Children

I urge you to be careful about fearful speech. We can fill our children with fear if our conversation is filled with fear. Even if the parent isn't speaking directly to the child, children are affected by what they hear. Here are some examples of things parents might say that could instill fear in their children without them intending for it to happen.

I am afraid if I let you drive to the party with your friends that you might have an accident and get hurt.

I would rather you not go to that party; I don't want you to get in trouble.

I don't want you to play football because it is a dangerous sport and I am afraid you will get injured.

I don't want you to play outside because there are bad people in the world who might take you away and hurt you.

Things are so bad in the world and I am afraid of what the
future holds.

I am afraid my kids will get hooked on drugs or get involved
with the wrong crowd.

I am afraid I may lose my job and then I don't know what we
will do.

Even saying that you dread things can hinder your children
from facing all things with a brave and courageous attitude. We
don't have to dread anything, especially simple things like clean-
ing the house, mowing the grass, or going to the grocery store. We
can face life with a passionate cour-
age that seeps into everything we do.
The more consistent your example is
to your children, the more effective
it will be.

> The more consistent your
> example is to your children,
> the more effective it will be.

There are some things that our children should be taught to be
cautious of, but only things that will definitely hurt them. Things
like touching a hot stove, walking into oncoming traffic, or jump-
ing off a cliff are good examples. Of course we need to teach caution, but we don't want to breed fear in them.

The Responsibility of Parenting

The privilege and responsibility of parenting are both tremendous. Let us not focus on the privilege and joys without focusing
also on the responsibility. One of the greatest responsibilities we
have is to consistently set a good, godly example for our children. Far too many parents tell their children what to do, but fail
to do it themselves. It is next to useless to teach your children
what they should do, and then show them the opposite of what

you have taught with words. Children are very intuitive, and they realize and absorb more than what we might think. So I highly recommend making a commitment to parenting by example. Jesus said that He came to set an example for us so we would do what He did (see John 13:15). What if God's Word taught us to be brave, but we saw example after example in Scripture of Jesus being fearful? I think you get the point I am attempting to make.

We can easily teach our children honesty, integrity, kindness, generosity, bravery, and a multitude of other good character traits by simply making a commitment to be a good example to them. Let's be willing to take a serious look at our behavior and ask ourselves if we want our children to do what we are doing. If so, then let's keep doing it, and if not, then let's change it with God's help. Even if making the change is difficult, let's do it because we love them.

CHAPTER 20

The Fear of Death

And also that He might deliver and completely set free all those who through the [haunting] fear of death were held in bondage throughout the whole course of their lives.

Hebrews 2:15

One of the greatest freedoms for the Christian is freedom from the fear of death. Although none of us want to die before our time, it doesn't need to frighten us if we believe that death simply means leaving this temporary home to go to our eternal home where we will see God face to face. It is often said that dying is like going through a revolving door. We are here on Earth, and then the moment we die, we are in God's presence if we are His children.

The word "death" is defined in the *Vine's Greek Dictionary* as *the separation of the soul (the spiritual part of man) from the body (the material part), the latter ceasing to function and turning to dust.* God's Word promises believers in Jesus Christ that they will ultimately have a new glorified body. I don't know about you, but I am looking forward to having one that has no wrinkles, no cellulite, no sagging chin or arms, and no pain or stiffness. When we think of dying, or of no longer being in this natural realm, we should think of what we will be gaining and not what we are losing.

Death does not mean that we cease to exist entirely, but we merely cease to exist in the form we are currently in. The most important part of us, the spiritual part, never ceases to exist.

The old saying, "The only thing you can really count on is death and taxes," is not the most comforting expression for someone who is afraid of death. The fear of death is a primal fear across the board for humanity unless one has been delivered from it through faith in God. God promises us eternal life through our faith in His Son Jesus Christ. As Christians, we can truthfully say, "I will live forever!" Your address will change someday from Earth to Heaven, but you will never really die. Actually, no person really dies. Their body will cease to exist, but the spirit and soul of each person will go somewhere after their time on Earth is up. I am grateful to have the hope of a beautiful, peaceful place where there will be no more tears, pain, or dying, and we will live in the actual presence of God.

> *God will wipe away every tear from their eyes; and death shall be no more, neither shall there be anguish (sorrow and mourning) nor grief nor pain any more, for the old conditions and the former order of things have passed away.*
>
> Revelation 21:4

Heaven, the eternal home of the believer in Jesus Christ, is described as not only totally peaceful, but it is stunningly beautiful according to descriptions in the Bible (see Revelation 21 and 22). Having faith that this is our destiny delivers us from the fear of death. Death is not an unknown nothingness, but a graduation into better things than what we have experienced on Earth.

The Apostle Paul Talks About Death

For me to live is Christ [His life in me], and to die is gain [the gain of the glory of eternity].

Philippians 1:21

Believers were persecuted every day, so Paul was always in danger of death. He was especially hated because of his aggressive role in leading people to salvation through faith in Christ. His bold, outspoken declaration of the need for all to be saved from their sin, including the Jew who viewed himself as religious and righteous, brought him a lot of severe persecution. Paul made it clear that because of the death and resurrection of Jesus, the Gentile was now equal with the Jew in God's eyes through grace (unmerited favor). This absolutely infuriated the Jews because they prided themselves in being closer to God than other people, and they sought to silence Paul. Paul was beaten, imprisoned, stoned, starved, and hunted by those who would have gladly killed him, and yet he seemed to have no fear of death.

Then Paul replied, What do you mean by weeping and breaking my heart like this? For I hold myself in readiness not only to be arrested and bound and imprisoned at Jerusalem, but also [even] to die for the name of the Lord Jesus.

Acts 21:13

Paul had a proper mind-set toward death. He knew that it was inevitable for him just as it is for all of us, and he purposed to not allow the fear of it to prevent him from fulfilling the will of God. It is rather pointless to fear something that we have no way of preventing. We must not let the fear of death prevent us from truly living! Paul knew that death simply meant that he would cease to exist in the body, but he was also assured that he would be resurrected

> *We must not let the fear of death prevent us from truly living!*

in a spiritual and better condition. That's why he encouraged the Church in 2 Corinthians 5:8 (KJV) by saying to "be absent from the body" is "to be present with the Lord."

Paul had more things to say to the Corinthians about death and resurrection. He explained to them that even when a seed is planted in the ground, it dies or ceases to exist as a seed, and then it is resurrected or comes out of the ground as something entirely different. A seed might be planted in the ground and a tomato may come out! We have our flesh-and-bone bodies and when they are planted in death, they too are resurrected in another and better form. Please read these Scripture verses and be assured that death on Earth only means the putting off of the physical body, but it does not mean that we cease to exist.

> *So it is with the resurrection of the dead. [The body] that is sown is perishable and decays, but [the body] that is resurrected is imperishable (immune to decay, immortal).*
>
> *It is sown in dishonor and humiliation; it is raised in honor and glory. It is sown in infirmity and weakness; it is resurrected in strength and endued with power.*
>
> *It is sown a natural (physical) body; it is raised a supernatural (a spiritual) body. [As surely as] there is a physical body, there is also a spiritual body.*
>
> 1 Corinthians 15:42–44

Death need not be feared when we receive by faith what God's Word says about it. Live your life fully and know that when your

time on Earth is ended, you will enter into a better life than you
ever had here.

God's Simple Plan

There are of course countless people who don't believe in the Christian doctrine of salvation and eternal life with God through faith
in Jesus Christ. Millions of people from various religions believe
in some form of reincarnation. They believe they will die and
then return in another form, but God says in His Word that it is
appointed once for man to die and then the judgment (see Hebrews
9:27). I read a little bit about reincarnation in preparation to write
this chapter, and to be honest, it makes me sad that some people
choose to believe in this confusing deception about eternity. Is it
possible that people believe in reincarnation simply because they
cannot face death? Perhaps it is an escape mechanism for them,
but I cannot help wondering how they truly feel at the moment of
death. Or for that matter, how does an atheist feel or an agnostic,
or an idol worshipper when they come face to face with death? The
Christian is the only one who can die in peace—the Christian can
even be enthusiastic about seeing God's face.

I have often said that it seems to me it would be better to believe
the Gospel than not to, because even if we are wrong (which we
are not), we haven't lost anything, but if the unbeliever is wrong,
he is doomed to eternal misery.

I am glad that faith in God's plan is simple. As a matter of fact,
God said that we must come as a little child and simply believe
what His Word teaches. If any person will look into God's Word
with their heart instead of their head, they will find faith there.
God gives us faith and it is up to us where we place it. Everyone
believes something. Even unbelief is a type of belief. Why not

make what you believe something that will produce good, peaceful, joyful, hopeful living? Believe that God loves you, has a wonderful plan for your life, and He wants to deliver you from all fear, including the fear of death.

> *Believe that God loves you, has a wonderful plan for your life, and He wants to deliver you from all fear, including the fear of death.*

The Resurrection

We have all sinned and come short of the glory of God, and sin demands the penalty of death. We could not pay the great debt we owed to God, so Jesus came from Heaven to Earth to reconcile us to God by paying for our sins and dying in our place. He took our punishment, and through great suffering and the spilling of His precious blood, He redeemed us (see Romans 3:23–25; Isaiah 53:4–5; Luke 23; 1 Peter 1:19).

But, thankfully, the story doesn't end with Jesus' death. On the third day after His death and burial, He was resurrected from the dead (see Luke 24). Death could not hold Him. He rose from the dead and is now seated at the right hand of God. Because death had no power over Him, it has no power over us either through our faith in Him.

The Muslims believe in the teachings of a prophet named Muhammad, who is dead. The Buddhist believes in the teachings of a man named Buddha, who is also dead. Many other religions base their faith on someone who is dead, but we believe in Jesus who is alive!

Is there any historical proof of the resurrection? There were numerous accounts from Christ's disciples of an empty tomb with the grave clothes left behind. There were also numerous eyewitness accounts of people seeing Jesus on Earth after His crucifixion. He appeared to them, ate with them, and talked with them. Historically speaking, the Bible has been proven to be accurate, and more evidence to that fact is being uncovered all the time. As true believers in Christ, historical proof only validates what we already know in our hearts to be true—Jesus is alive! And because He lives, we never need to fear death.

The fear of death actually has a name like most fears do. It is "thanatophobia," and it is a phobia rather than a simple fear that one might experience occasionally. In my opinion, faith in God's Word and belief in the fact that Jesus rose from the dead is the way to be free from the haunting fear of death. If we believe that our sins are forgiven, we are placed in right standing with God through our faith in Jesus Christ, and we will see God face-to-face the moment we die, so what is there to fear?

William Randolph Hearst built the great Hearst Castle near Morro Bay. He filled the structure with the most beautiful objects and art of our world. Yet whenever anyone visited, he had a standing rule that no guest in his home could ever mention the word "death." Each night, he was afraid to go to sleep because he was tormented by the fear of death.[1]

Mr. Hearst's fear of death did not prevent him from dying. It was a negative emotion and wrong mind-set that stole his joy of living, and he ultimately had to face his greatest fear anyway.

I am sure his story is only representative of the stories of multitudes of people who are tormented continually by the fear of death. But here is another story about a Christian man and his faith in God.

Seeking to know God better, John Chrysostom became a hermit in the mountains near Antioch in AD 373. Although his

time of isolation was cut short by illness, he learned that
with God at his side, he could stand alone against anyone
or anything. That lesson served Chrysostom well. In AD 398
he was appointed patriarch of Constantinople, where his
zeal for reform antagonized the Empress Eudoxia, who had
him exiled. Allowed to return after a short time, Chrysostom
again infuriated Eudoxia, who sent him away again. How did
Chrysostom respond to such persecution? With these words:
"What can I fear? Will it be death? But you know that Christ
is my life, and that I shall gain by death. Will it be exile? But
the earth and all its fullness are the Lord's. Poverty I do not
fear; riches I do not sigh for; and from death I do not shrink."[2]

The depth of faith that a person has in God determines whether
or not they will fear death. John Chrysostom knew his God, and
he trusted His promises; therefore, he had nothing to fear—not
even death.

The Fear of Dying

Perhaps the fear of dying is actually greater than the fear of death.
I was once in an airplane that lost oxygen pressure in the cabin
and the pilots had to nose-dive from 30,000 feet to 10,000 feet
so we would have breathable air. They were in action mode and
couldn't take time to tell us what was happening. We could feel
the plane rapidly losing altitude and we saw the pilots with their
oxygen on...a little spooky to say the least! I remember thinking, *Well Lord, I may be coming home, but I wonder if this is going*
to hurt! I wasn't concerned about being dead, but I was a bit concerned about dying and what it might take to do it.

Sickness, disease, and often a long and painful process may

precede death, and none of us would look forward to that. I am sure like me, you may pray that when your time comes to leave Earth you will just go to sleep one night and then wake up in Heaven. My thought is, "You have not because you ask not" (see James 4:2), so why not ask for something painless? However, we can be assured that whatever it takes to get out of this world, God will enable us to do it without fear.

All fear is rooted in wrong belief systems or thought habits, and I believe we can change them with God's help. Learning to trust God to take care of us is the ultimate answer to freedom from the fear of dying. I cannot promise that dying will be painless because like you, I haven't experienced it yet. However, I do believe I can say with confidence that God will be with us and He will give us the grace we need at the time we need it. I have met amazing people going through very painful sicknesses who always have a smile and a kind word for others. When I have asked how they can do it, without fail, they say, "It is the grace of God."

Whether the process of my dying is short or long, painful or painless, I trust that God will give me what I need to do it gracefully. Because of that trust, I have peace about it. If you are not enjoying that peace, I pray you will take to heart the things you are reading and realize that you need not fear the unknown. We should remember that Jesus has gone before us to prepare the way, and He has promised to never leave us nor forsake us (see Hebrews 13:5; Matthew 28:20). He is with us in life and He will be with us in death.

> *Do not let your hearts be troubled (distressed, agitated). You*
> *believe in and adhere to and trust in and rely on God; believe*
> *in and adhere to and trust in and rely also on Me.*

In My Father's house there are many dwelling places (homes).
If it were not so, I would have told you; for I am going away to
prepare a place for you.

And when (if) I go and make ready a place for you, I will
come back again and will take you to Myself, that where I am
you may be also.

John 14:1–3

I have heard many, many stories of people on their deathbeds saying, "Jesus is here for me now. I have to go." Or, "I see the light and I must follow it." My life has been beautiful, and I want my death to be beautiful also. I believe we can prepare for death properly by simply not being afraid of it. We are all going to have to do it eventually, so why not do it afraid?

CHAPTER 21

Do It Afraid!

Courage doesn't always roar; sometimes courage is the little voice at the end of the day that says, "I'll try again tomorrow."

Mary Anne Radmacher

Fear is an enemy that torments the soul and seeks to steal our life. Conquering it is not something that we do in one day, or even in 1,000 days. It is something that we conquer one day at a time. I am writing the book, and I still confront and deal with fear…little, annoying fears that try to make me think I need to do more, or try harder, or be nicer. Fear can show up quite unexpectedly in many ways. One of our goals should be to recognize it so we can deal with it promptly.

Just this week I was waking up at about 2 or 3 in the morning and then having difficulty going back to sleep. After two nights of that, I found myself going to bed with a vague sort of fear that it would happen again, and sure enough it did. After about three nights of the same thing, God reminded me that I could pray and resist Satan, the source of all fear. According to God's Word, the sleep of the righteous should be sweet (see Proverbs 3:24). I prayed immediately and went back to sleep and have not had any problems since then. If you have difficulty thinking about rebuking or resisting Satan, let me remind you that Jesus did it, and

His example is always good enough for me. We have power and authority over the enemy, but authority is useless if it is not exercised.

> We have power and authority over the enemy, but authority is useless if it is not exercised.

Being free from fear doesn't mean that we will never experience it or be confronted by it. It means that we are committed to not allowing it to rule our lives, and when necessary we will do what we need to do, even if we have to do it afraid.

The truth is that reading this book may stir up the fears you have. It may make you more aware of them and hopefully more determined to confront them. Simply reading a book about something doesn't mean we have no responsibility to apply the principles we have read about. Knowing about something has no value if we don't do something with the knowledge we have. Wisdom is the proper use of knowledge. I have tried to impart most of what I have learned about fear over the past 38 years. I have given you information, but what you really need is *revelation*. Revelation comes as we pray about a truth we have heard, meditate on it, and put the principles to work in our life that we have learned.

I think one of our biggest mistakes in life can be to think that we should have victory in an area merely because we read a book or hear a message about something. James said that if we are hearers of the Word and not doers, we are like someone who looks at himself in a mirror and goes away and forgets what he looks like (see James 1:22–24).

If you are reading this chapter, I am assuming you have almost completed the book and I urge you not to put it back on your bookshelf and merely be proud that you have completed yet another book about God and His ways, and then go away and think, *Now I know all about fear.*

Knowing something mentally and knowing it by experience are two entirely different things. We often say that heart knowledge is much deeper than head knowledge. A thing gets into our heart as we exercise it, not just when we theorize about it. Each fear that you confront becomes a small victory for you and it prepares you to face the next one. Each time you feel fear and decide to "do it afraid," you will enjoy your new freedom so much that you will soon be totally unwilling to do without it. You will soon be determined that your days of slavery to fear are over. That does not mean that you won't still need to confront fear, but it does mean that you will be more and more determined to keep confronting it.

> Each fear that you confront becomes a small victory for you and it prepares you to face the next one.

We all know from reading books and hearing wonderful sermons that no matter how much we need or enjoy them, it is easy to forget them. There are some books and teachings that we need to not forget on our bookshelves, but we should keep them nearby so we can refer to them often. I have reread some of the books that have meant a great deal to me several times, and there are certain sections of books that I go back and read over and over anytime I feel I am getting weak in an area.

> *In [this] freedom Christ has made us free [and completely liberated us]; stand fast then, and do not be hampered and held ensnared and submit again to a yoke of slavery [which you have once put off].*
>
> Galatians 5:1

This Scripture is very clear that even though we have been completely liberated from a yoke of slavery, we will need at times to "stand fast" and not allow ourselves to be entrapped by it again.

Satan is very shrewd and he doesn't give up easily. I guess we can say that he never completely gives up the hope of drawing us back into bondage. We must live watchfully, ready to recognize and immediately confront the things that steal our liberty in Christ.

When You Fall, Get Up and Keep Going!

The Bible says that the righteous man falls seven times and gets up again (see Proverbs 24:16). I love that Scripture and I am greatly encouraged by it. Even the most righteous person fails to do everything he knows to do all the time, but he is committed to not giving up. Just because you have a weak moment, that doesn't mean you have lost your victory. If we give up even God can't help us because we receive His help through faith, not through hopelessness. We need to stay positive, hopeful, and filled with faith, and when we do there is nothing we cannot overcome. I often say that anyone can succeed if they refuse to give up!

Some fears are more deeply rooted in us than other ones are, and for that reason they may be ones we will need to be more aggressive against. Mine is the fear of making people angry. My father was always angry, and I never really knew if I had done something to make him that way or not. The fear of making my father angry was constantly with me throughout my childhood, and I still find today that if I am around some family member who seems to be upset or angry, I start wondering if I did anything to make that person angry. I would like to be able to say that after all these years of teaching others I no longer have to deal with this one fear, but the good news is that I do recognize it and I do deal with, so I still have the victory.

Being able to recognize the lies, deceit, and strategies of the devil is a major victory. We should always be ready to resist him at the onset of his attacks. The longer we let a fear remain, the more difficult it may be to get rid of. So make a decision to be a person of action. Laziness, passivity, and irresponsibility are an open invitation for Satan to rule you. In Matthew chapter 25, we are told of 10 virgins who went to meet the bridegroom. Five of them were foolish and got tired of waiting and fell asleep, the other five were wise and they stayed awake and continued their preparation to meet the bridegroom. Jesus said to them, "Be cautious and active because you don't know the day nor the hour when the Son of Man will come" (see Matthew 25:1–13).

I don't think it would be wrong to also say, "Be cautious and active because you don't know when the devil will attack with fear, or anything else he can do to keep you from God's wonderful plan for your life."

You Are Armed and Dangerous

Knowledge prepares us for the battle. You have what it takes to win. Actually, the Word of God says that we are more than conquerors through Christ who loves us (see Romans 8:37). You are armed with the truth of God's Word, and you are dangerous to the devil as long as you continue lifting up the shield of faith and actively applying the truth that you now have knowledge of.

God's Word arms us for battle. There is a war to be won, and we must see ourselves as soldiers in God's great army. You have the breastplate of righteousness, the belt of truth that is the Word of God, the helmet of salvation, the sword of the Spirit (God's Word), the shoes of peace, and the shield of faith. And to add to this, we have the power and privilege of prayer (see Ephesians

6:13–18). How can we be defeated? We cannot as long as we put on the armor that God supplies rather than storing it on a shelf somewhere and thinking that God will take care of us while we are inactive and passive.

With all of my heart I want you to believe that you already have the victory through Christ, and with His help (grace), you can apply that victory daily. God has given us all that we could ever need through Christ. He has blessed us with every blessing in the spiritual realm (see Ephesians 1:3). He has given us power and authority over all the power the devil possesses (see Luke 10:19). We have what it takes, but we must be active and never give up. Remember, a fall is not a failure! The righteous man falls seven times, and still he gets up again!

> With all of my heart I want you to believe that you already have the victory through Christ, and with His help (grace), you can apply that victory daily.

It Is Time to Possess the Land

In the Old Testament, God promised the Israelites that they could live in a place He called the Promised Land, a land that flowed with every good thing they would need to be fruitful and enjoy life. He also told them they would have to possess the land. He gave it and they had to possess it! The same thing is true for us today. Jesus has purchased with His own blood our freedom and every good thing we could ever desire, but we must possess it.

When we study the word "possess," we find it means to possess by dispossessing the current occupants. That sheds much light on what is required to live in the freedom that has been provided for us. We must be determined, alert, and unwilling to settle for anything less than complete victory.

Be well-balanced (temperate, sober of mind), be vigilant
and cautious at all times; for that enemy of yours, the devil,
roams around like a lion roaring [in fierce hunger], seeking
someone to seize upon and devour.

   Withstand him; be firm in faith [against his onset—rooted,
established, strong, immovable, and determined] . . .

1 Peter 5:8–9

When I first began to understand the amazing life that Jesus had provided for me, I felt angry that I had been robbed of it through deception. I was also a bit miffed that after many years of regular church attendance, I had not been clearly informed of what was mine through Jesus. I had been told what to do, but not how to do it! I pray I never make that mistake as a teacher of God's Word. I want to help people, not frustrate them.

I was a frustrated believer in Jesus who had very little—if any—victory in my daily life. I had assurance of Heaven, but no joy in living. I had no idea what was in my heavenly account; therefore, I lived as a bankrupt believer.

When I began to seriously study God's Word and found out what was mine, I didn't realize that the devil would oppose me every step of the way. Paul told Timothy to be prepared to "fight the good fight of faith" and "lay hold of eternal life" (see 1 Timothy 6:12). Eternal life does not merely refer to going to Heaven when we die. It begins the moment that we receive Jesus as Savior and Lord, and means life as God lives it. That sounds exciting! I want that kind of freedom and enjoyment, and I am unwilling to do without it. What about you?

Thank God, I finally saw the light and now know that although Satan will resist my freedom aggressively, I do have the power and authority to dispossess him and possess what is mine in Christ, and you do too.

Possessing the full freedom that is yours in Christ is a journey. There is always new ground to take. Learning how to confront fear is one of the very important things we need to learn because fear is one of the main tools of the devil.

Pay Attention to Your Thoughts and Feelings

Take a week and purposely pay attention to any fearful thoughts or feelings you might have. I believe when you realize how often fear comes against you, you will be surprised and appalled. But please remember that just because you feel fear does not mean you have to bow down to it. Recognizing fear is a good thing because you can simply smile and say, "No fear lives here!" You can do it afraid!

Pay attention even in little things. My hair is a little bit too long right now, and when it is, I have more difficulty getting it to look right. Today I have an important meeting and of course, like any woman, I want to look good. I found myself thinking, *I am concerned that I won't be able to get my hair to look good.* Does that qualify as a fear? Maybe it is not a full-blown fear, but it certainly isn't faith, so I decided to ask God to help me, and I am expecting it to look great!

Tomorrow I have a four-hour mentoring session, and 20 seasoned women in ministry will be asking me any question they want to ask, and of course I am supposed to answer them. Will I have all the answers, and will they be right answers? I can be afraid that I won't and will end up looking foolish, or I can go in faith believing that God will give me what I need when I need it.

My back is aching a little and I am out of town and can't get to my chiropractor. I have had some major back issues in the past, so it might be easy for me to accept the fear that they are starting again. I choose to believe it is due to sleeping in a different bed, and I will do some exercises for my back muscles and have a good day.

I am offering these simple examples so you can see that all fears are not huge ones. Many of them are vague, nagging little thoughts that prevent us from fully enjoying life. If you are ready to confront fear, you may as well confront all of it!

Don't be impatient. Possessing freedom is an ongoing process. It is something we gain and then need to maintain. Always look at and enjoy your progress instead of merely looking at how far you have to go. Today is a new day, and every new day is a day to begin again. Thank you for allowing me to share with you what I have learned about confronting fear by doing it afraid, and remember the quote at the beginning of this chapter: "Courage doesn't always roar; sometimes courage is the little voice at the end of the day that says, 'I'll try again tomorrow.'"

*I sought (inquired of) the Lord and required Him
[of necessity and on the authority of His Word], and
He heard me, and delivered me from all my fears.*
Psalm 34:4

*For God did not give us a spirit of timidity (of cowardice,
of craven and cringing and fawning fear), but [He has given
us a spirit] of power and of love and of calm and
well-balanced mind and discipline and self-control.*
2 Timothy 1:7

*For [the Spirit which] you have now received [is] not a spirit
of slavery to put you once more in bondage to fear, but you
have received the Spirit of adoption [the Spirit producing sonship]
in [the bliss of] which we cry, Abba (Father)! Father!*
Romans 8:15

*Have not I commanded you? Be strong, vigorous,
and very courageous. Be not afraid, neither be dismayed,
for the Lord your God is with you wherever you go.*
Joshua 1:9

Casting the whole of your care [all your anxieties, all your worries,
all your concerns, once and for all] on Him, for He cares for you
affectionately and cares about you watchfully.
1 Peter 5:7

There is no fear in love; but perfect love casts out fear, because
fear involves torment. But he who fears has not been made
perfect in love. We love Him because He first loved us.
1 John 4:18–19 (NKJV)

The Lord is my Light and my Salvation—whom shall
I fear or dread? The Lord is the Refuge and Stronghold
of my life—of whom shall I be afraid?
Psalm 27:1

Fear not [there is nothing to fear], for I am with you;
do not look around you in terror and be dismayed, for I am
your God. I will strengthen and harden you to difficulties, yes,
I will help you; yes, I will hold you up and retain you with
My [victorious] right hand of rightness and justice.
Isaiah 41:10

For I the Lord your God hold your right hand; I am the Lord,
Who says to you, Fear not; I will help you!
Isaiah 41:13

I have told you these things, so that in Me you may have
[perfect] peace and confidence. In the world you have
tribulation and trials and distress and frustration; but be
of good cheer [take courage; be confident, certain, undaunted]!

*For I have overcome the world. [I have deprived it of
power to harm you and have conquered it for you.]*
John 16:33

*Yes, though I walk through the [deep, sunless] valley of the
shadow of death, I will fear or dread no evil, for You are with me;
Your rod [to protect] and Your staff [to guide], they comfort me.*
Psalm 23:4

*The Lord will fight for you, and you shall hold
your peace and remain at rest.*
Exodus 14:14

*What time I am afraid, I will have confidence in and
put my trust and reliance in You. By [the help of] God I will
praise His word; on God I lean, rely, and confidently put my trust;
I will not fear. What can man, who is flesh, do to me?*
Psalm 56:3–4

*It is the Lord Who goes before you; He will [march] with you;
He will not fail you or let you go or forsake you; [let there be no
cowardice or flinching, but] fear not, neither become broken
[in spirit—depressed, dismayed, and unnerved with alarm].*
Deuteronomy 31:8

*So we take comfort and are encouraged and
confidently and boldly say, The Lord is my Helper;
I will not be seized with alarm [I will not fear or dread
or be terrified]. What can man do to me?*
Hebrews 13:6

Peace I leave with you; My [own] peace I now give and
bequeath to you. Not as the world gives do I give to you. Do not
let your hearts be troubled, neither let them be afraid. [Stop allowing
yourselves to be agitated and disturbed; and do not permit yourselves
to be fearful and intimidated and cowardly and unsettled.]
John 14:27

Keep and protect me, O God, for in You I have found refuge,
and in You do I put my trust and hide myself.
Psalm 16:1

But Jesus came and touched them and said, Get up,
and do not be afraid.
Matthew 17:7

Do not fret or have any anxiety about anything,
but in every circumstance and in everything, by prayer
and petition (definite requests), with thanksgiving,
continue to make your wants known to God.
Philippians 4:6

You shall not fear them, for the Lord your God shall fight for you.
Deuteronomy 3:22

Now faith is the substance of things hoped for,
the evidence of things not seen.
Hebrews 11:1 (NKJV)

So faith comes by hearing [what is told], and what is heard
comes by the preaching [of the message that came from the lips]
of Christ (the Messiah Himself).
Romans 10:17

…For truly I say to you, if you have faith [that is living]
like a grain of mustard seed, you can say to this mountain,
Move from here to yonder place, and it will move;
and nothing will be impossible to you.
Matthew 17:20

For with God nothing is ever impossible and no word from
God shall be without power or impossible of fulfillment.
Luke 1:37

So that your faith might not rest in the wisdom of men
(human philosophy), but in the power of God.
1 Corinthians 2:5

*And whoever continues to live and believes in
(has faith in, cleaves to, and relies on) Me shall never
[actually] die at all. Do you believe this?*
John 11:26

*For it is by free grace (God's unmerited favor) that you are
saved (delivered from judgment and made partakers of Christ's
salvation) through [your] faith. And this [salvation] is not of
yourselves [of your own doing, it came not through your own
striving], but it is the gift of God.*
Ephesians 2:8

*But without faith it is impossible to please and be
satisfactory to Him. For whoever would come near to God
must [necessarily] believe that God exists and that He is the
rewarder of those who earnestly and diligently seek Him [out].*
Hebrews 11:6

*He said to them, Why are you so timid and fearful?
How is it that you have no faith (no firmly relying trust)?*
Mark 4:40

*And whatever you ask for in prayer, having faith
and [really] believing, you will receive.*
Matthew 21:22

*And he [Abram] believed in (trusted in, relied on,
remained steadfast to) the Lord, and He counted it to
him as righteousness (right standing with God).*
Genesis 15:6

*...Blessed and happy and to be envied are those
who have never seen Me and yet have believed and adhered
to and trusted and relied on Me.*
John 20:29

*The apostles said to the Lord, Increase our faith (that trust
and confidence that spring from our belief in God).*
Luke 17:5

For in Christ Jesus you are all sons of God through faith.
Galatians 3:26

*But someone will say, "You have faith, and I have works."
Show me your faith without your works, and I will show
you my faith by my works.*
James 2:18 (NKJV)

*Look at the proud; his soul is not straight or right within him,
but the [rigidly] just and the [uncompromisingly] righteous
man shall live by his faith and in his faithfulness.*
Habakkuk 2:4

*And Jesus said to him, Receive your sight! Your faith (your trust and
confidence that spring from your faith in God) has healed you.*
Luke 18:42

*Commit your way to the Lord [roll and repose each care of
your load on Him]; trust (lean on, rely on, and be confident)
also in Him and He will bring it to pass.*
Psalm 37:5

*Fight the good fight of the faith; lay hold of the eternal
life to which you were summoned and [for which] you confessed
the good confession [of faith] before many witnesses.*
1 Timothy 6:12

*For whatever is born of God is victorious over the world;
and this is the victory that conquers the world, even our faith.*
1 John 5:4

Chapter 1: Say Good-Bye to Fear

1 www.moreillustrations.com

Chapter 4: Phobias

1 http://www.mayoclinic.com/health/phobias/DS00272
2 Information provided by Jordan Smoller—Associate Professor of Psychiatry at Harvard Medical School and Associate Professor in the Department of Epidemiology at the Harvard School of Public Health. Author of *The Other Side of Normal*. (Source: http://www.huffingtonpost.com/jordan -smoller/biggest-phobias_b_1525627.html)
3 http://animal.discovery.com/tv/my-extreme-animal-phobia/top-10-weirdest -phobias.html
4 www.family-times.net/illustrations/fear/
5 Lloyd C. Douglas, *Magnificent Obsession* (New York, New York: Houghton Mifflin Company, 1929), 5.
6 http://www.statisticbrain.com/fear-phobia-statistics/

Chapter 5: Cultivating Courage

1 Paul Harvey, Los Angeles Times Syndicate

Chapter 11: The Fear of Not Being Wanted

1 Nelson's Annual Preacher's Sourcebook: 2003 Edition, p. 385
2 http://en.thinkexist.com/quotation/true_success_is_overcoming_the _fear_of_being/218403.html

Chapter 12: The Fear of Being Inadequate

1 http://www.sermoncentral.com/sermons/facing-your-fear-of-failure-jonathan -mcleod-sermon-on-fear-and-worry-89976.asp
2 http://www.brainyquote.com/quotes/quotes/m/michaeljor127660.html
3 http://www.inspirational-quotes.info/failure.html

4 http://www.henryfordquotes.org/one-who-fears-failure-limits-his-activi ties-failure-is-only-the-opportunity-to-more-intelligently-begin-again/

Chapter 14: The Fear of Man

1 Sunday School Chronicle, www.moreillustrations.com

Chapter 16: The Fear of Making Mistakes

1 Taken from Alina Tugend, *New York Times*, "The Paralyzing Problem of Too Many Choices."

Chapter 19: Are You Passing Your Fears on to Your Children?

1 Found at www.a-better-child.org/page/889398

Chapter 20: The Fear of Death

1 http://www.heartlight.org/cgi/simplify.cgi?20050225_feardeath.html

2 Today in the Word, MBI, October 1991, p.33

JOYCE MEYER is one of the world's leading practical Bible teachers. Her TV and radio broadcast, *Enjoying Everyday Life*, airs on hundreds of television networks and radio stations worldwide.

Joyce has written more than 100 inspirational books. Her bestsellers include *Power Thoughts; The Confident Woman; Look Great, Feel Great; Starting Your Day Right; Ending Your Day Right; Approval Addiction; How to Hear from God; Beauty for Ashes;* and *Battlefield of the Mind.*

Joyce travels extensively, holding conferences throughout the year, speaking to thousands around the world.

Joyce Meyer Ministries
P.O. Box 655
Fenton, MO 63026
USA
(636) 349-0303

Joyce Meyer Ministries—Canada
P.O. Box 7700
Vancouver, BC V6B 4E2
Canada
(800) 868-1002

Joyce Meyer Ministries—Australia
Locked Bag 77
Mansfield Delivery Centre
Queensland 4122
Australia
(07) 3349 1200

Joyce Meyer Ministries—England
P.O. Box 1549
Windsor SL4 1GT
United Kingdom
01753 831102

Joyce Meyer Ministries—South Africa
P.O. Box 5
Cape Town 8000
South Africa
(27) 21-701-1056

Starting Your Day Right
Straight Talk
Teenagers Are People Too!
Trusting God Day by Day
The Word, the Name, the Blood
Woman to Woman
You Can Begin Again

*Study Guide available for this title